Book. Blog. Broadcast.

The Trifecta of
Entrepreneurial Success

Other Titles by Connie Ragen Green

Book. Blog. Broadcast.

The Trifecta of Entrepreneurial Success

By
Connie Ragen Green

Copyright © 2015 by Hunter's Moon Publishing

 ISBN Paperback: 978-1-937988-24-1
ISBN Kindle: 978-1-937988-25-8

Hunter's Moon Publishing
http://HuntersMoonPublishing.com

Interior Design by Geoff Hoff
Cover Design by Geoff Hoff

Dedication

Stay hungry, stay foolish.
~ Steve Jobs

Making the leap from a life that is comfortable, even if it isn't exactly as you had hoped it would be, into a life filled with risk and the possibility of adversity and the unknown at every turn can be daunting, but if you have the entrepreneurial spirit living inside of you then it is something you absolutely must do in order to be true to yourself.

I am dedicating this book to all of the entrepreneurs of the world, whether or not they are living their dream or still working to make that happen in their lives. To those who are reinventing themselves, discovering their creative side, and exploring new paradigms for creating income and enjoying success, this book is intended as a blueprint for you.

"Think different" was an advertising slogan for Apple, Inc. (then Apple Computer, Inc.) in 1997. The creative concept and the slogan "Think different" were created by art director Craig Tanimoto. The slogan has been widely taken as a response to IBM's motto "Think". This was turned into a commercial for network television, and two versions were created before it first aired: one with actor Richard Dreyfuss voicing the narrative portion, and one with a Steve Jobs voiceover. At the last moment Jobs chose to air the one with Dreyfuss' voice because he felt like the commercial shouldn't be about him but about the company. The copy for this had been written by creative director Rob Siltanen and copywriter Ken Segall.

Here is the full text, and if you can relate to this in any way then you are in the right place.

Here's to the crazy ones, the misfits, the rebels, the troublemakers, the round pegs in the square holes... the ones who see things differently - they're not fond of rules... You can quote them, disagree with them, glorify or vilify them, but the only thing you can't do is ignore them because they change things... they push the human race forward, and while some may see them as the crazy ones, we see genius, because the ones who are crazy enough to think that they can change the world, are the ones who do.

Dare to be who you feel you truly are as a human being. Be willing to go where you have never gone and to do what you have never done in order to serve your inner being and feed your soul. Allow yourself the freedom to get caught up in the exhilarating vortex of life. But most of all, live every day as though it could be your last by just being yourself.

Connie Ragen Green

Table of Contents

Foreword

*There is nothing to writing. All you do is
sit down at a typewriter and bleed.*
~ Ernest Hemingway

I have written my entire life, from the time I was quite young. I wrote my first full short story when I was nine. My mother proudly kept the handwritten manuscript in the front of her huge Random House dictionary until the day she died. Actually, it's probably still there. She kept it even though, in the story, the main character's mother had died a horrible death. (What young boy hasn't fantasized about that? Mothers can be quite forgiving of their youngsters' angst.)

Since then, I've written stories, poems, stage plays and screen plays, articles, web series, novels. I've written for myself and in collaboration with others. I've written as a ghost writer. I've written science fiction and horror and psychological drama and humor (some smart and some very, very silly.) I've written sales copy (again, for myself and for others) and blog posts. And, of course, I've written how-to and business books and books on creativity and on writing. Because I've always written, it used to seem to me that anyone could just sit down and do it. In the last several years, I've realized this often isn't so. Many people have such a resistance to even the thought of writing that they find they are absolutely incapable of doing it. Even thinking about considering it will make their palms sticky and then break out in a bad case of the vapors. Or, for the less dramatic among us, make them immediately think of something easier and more pleasant, like wrestling a giant squid without a wet suit or oxygen tank at a thousand feet below the surface of the ocean. No matter how you view it, though, I say you can get over that fear.

Now let me tell you about Connie Ragen Green.

For many years, Connie was a school teacher. She taught her students how to write. That was ironic, because she herself always wanted to write, but never did. That is true for a lot of people. Partly, I imagine, it's out of fear, giant squids notwithstanding – what if I'm just not very good – and partly out of inertia. Then, when she left school teaching behind and started her online information business, she realized she actually needed to write. You couldn't create information products without at least some writing. So she did. She wrote blog posts and articles and created those information products. Her early work, by her own admission, wasn't very good, but she kept at it, early on accepting a challenge to write 100 articles in 100 days. I understand she beat the challenge by several days. The more she wrote, the better her writing became. She has now written or contributed to at least fifteen books and has published at least one of her own a year for the last six years. She has many hundreds of articles published, and even more blog posts on her own and others' blogs.

I call myself a writer. Connie puts me to shame.

Connie proves that, if you decide you can write, you can. Will it be brilliant? Probably not at first. (And if you're gunning for brilliance every time you sit down to write, you will create a barrier to writing that even William Shakespeare wouldn't be able to surmount.)

I first met Connie five or six years ago in an online coaching group that met on a webinar every Tuesday night. We met in person shortly after that, at a live event put on by Pat O'Bryan, the fellow who ran the online group. We had both been online for about the same amount of time, but

Connie was already making her living (and it was already a good living!) with her online business, and I had yet to crack that code. Well, seek and ye shall find.

We started working together in various capacities and created some courses together. During this time, and in large part because of her mentoring and friendship, my business became more and more successful. Then one day, she called me up and said, "Let's write a book together. I'll write about confidence and you write about creativity." One doesn't say no to an offer like that, and *The Inner Game of Internet Marketing* was born.

A year or so later, Connie called and said, "Let's write another book. About time management. And we'll do it in a week. And part of the book will be about the process of writing the book." I'm up for a ridiculous challenge. That became *Time Management Strategies for Entrepreneurs*. Ask and it shall be given.

It would be easy to feel intimidated by Connie; she is amazingly productive, committed and disciplined. However, when you remember that she started not believing she could write (and spent many years not writing because of that) then, once it became obvious it was the only choice, just sat down and started, it is easier to become inspired rather than intimidated.

If you're reading this book, you have at least considered the possibility that you might want to be an entrepreneur. If you want to be an entrepreneur, you have to at least consider that writing will be part of it. Take Connie as your example and follow her lead. She started out not thinking she could write. Then she wrote. A lot. Now, she has tons of books, several blogs and has "broadcast" her way out into the world with Podcasts, on social media, through business organizations and networks and through philanthropic and charitable works. Connie has taken it to a degree you may or may not want to get to: She has lots of products, clients all over the world, a private premium

Book. Blog. Broadcast.

mentoring program, does business consultation for large corporations and gives a couple of live events every year where she shares the latest stuff she's up to. Not to mention that she publishes a lot of books. And, with all of this, she still has time to enjoy herself, visit family in Europe, travel to Central America, watch a movie or play once in a while and play with her dogs. Knock, and the door shall be open.

Everyone has something to say. Everyone has something they know about that others want to learn. Everyone has stories to tell, whether they're true to life, completely fictional, "how-to," educational or anything else you could name. And by everyone, I mean you. Be inspired by Connie's journey. Learn how she did it. Follow her lead. Once you start being in the habit of writing regularly, you can create your own path. Then you, too, can experience the Trifecta of entrepreneurial success: *Book. Blog. Broadcast.*

Let's all give Connie a run for her money. You don't have to call yourself a writer, like I do. You just have to write. Like Connie does.

Geoff Hoff
Los Angeles
September, 2015

Preface

All of our dreams can come true, if we
have the courage to pursue them.
~ Walt Disney

I was the last person in the world anyone could have imagined would become a successful entrepreneur. During the majority of my adult life and up until the age of fifty, I worked as a classroom teacher at four different schools, teaching the gamut of ages from Kindergarten through high school, and even two years of evening classes at an adult school. For the first ten years this was a calling, something I loved as much as life itself. After that the real world moved closer, and after dealing with cancer on more than one occasion as well as a serious work injury I was ready to resign myself to the fact that teaching was simply a job.

For all of these years I was the controversial one at school, almost always believing that I had a "better idea" of how to convey knowledge and educate my students. Many hours were spent in preparing lessons that would empower them to think outside of the box as to what was truly possible for their own lives and in the world. The administration crushed my ideas most of the time, but every once in awhile they allowed me to do some activity that changed all of our lives for the better.

One of these projects was brought to our school initially by an inner city dance troupe from Los Angeles. They called themselves JUICE, and for ninety minutes every other

Thursday afternoon for six weeks my students were transformed into hip-hop dancers. It was fun and life changing for all of us. The young people who ran this program were brilliant in every way and this was a revolutionary experience for all of us.

It wasn't my imagination when I saw my kids walking taller, feeling and acting more confident, and happier to have some of the weight of the world lifted off of their shoulders. This dance class made a difference to each of them. If only we had had the opportunity to partake of more of these types of experiences over my twenty years in the classroom, everything would have been different. Enhancing the experience of the human condition is a worthwhile goal.

Simultaneously, I had been running my own real estate business for more years than I had been a teacher. As a broker and residential appraiser I helped people buy, sell, borrow, and invest in real estate as a way to change their living conditions and financial futures. This business definitely had its ups and downs over the three decades I worked at it seriously, but the contrast between that world and the world of teaching was one that led to a change in my mindset during the spring of 2005.

It was at that point in time that I made the conscious decision to change my life forever. Soon to turn fifty years old, I felt that I had to take action if I were to find out what the world could be like for me if I had the time and the money to explore the possibilities. With no children at home to support, I spent a year planning my escape.

Part of my new life included attending a variety of events. One of these, something from a group called Peak Potentials, was a Warrior Camp where we were divided into tribes of about thirty people each. Over the next three days we spent time in a sweat lodge (this is a purification ceremony held in a hut, typically dome-shaped and made with natural materials, and used by indigenous peoples of the Americas for ceremonial steam baths and prayer), climbed to heights of forty feet above the ground in a Swiss tree house to engage in a variety of balancing and endurance activities, and hiked through a local mountain range for ten hours, carrying logs and bricks. Our group also included a man with Down's syndrome, and being responsible for him added to our experience in a way I could never have imagined. I was transformed over those three days and came away with a greater desire to improve and change my life.

The information contained in this book comes from what I have learned and observed after leaving the security of a paycheck and commissions and fees from real estate and jumped feet first into the world of entrepreneurship. As an entrepreneur, you are responsible for making things happen. No one is going to call you up, knock on your door, or message you on Facebook to offer you a new opportunity; unlimited opportunities await you in the recesses of your mind. And just as the professional athlete does not go on vacation to get away from sports, your business is with you in every moment, whether waking or asleep. It can be simultaneously exhilarating, frustrating, and satisfying, and this can bring a cacophony of emotion to crash down upon you like waves to the shore. I can't imagine my life in any other way.

Whether you are brand new to this world, or have already dabbled and wish to take it to the next level, you will find my three-pronged strategy of writing and publishing a full length book, setting up and maintaining a blog, and broadcasting through audios and videos to be one that will not only take you out of your comfort zone but will catapult you into the spotlight for now and eternity.

I wasn't necessarily looking for an easy way to build a business; I was looking for a blueprint of sorts that could help the students in my Online Marketing Incubator move quickly from where they were as new entrepreneurs to closer to being thought of and respected as experts and authorities on their chosen topics.

The results have been nothing short of phenomenal for people all around the world and in a variety of niches; speaking engagements, bestselling books, businesses that continue to grow beyond expectations, and so much more. They took the advice I shared with them to heart and slowly incorporated these ideas into their souls. As they used this "Trifecta" of writing a full length book, setting up and maintaining an engaging blog, and hosting podcasts, recording videos, and speaking on their topic, it all came together for them in a seamless way. Others continue to join me in my Incubator and emulate the actions that lead to results.

This is a book that you don't simply read; you "do". Take notes, stop and daydream about how it will fit into your own business, and then take action. You are in a unique and enviable position at this point in time because of the work done by the pioneers of online marketing who came before us. The technology is more user-friendly, content creation has been refined, and social media gives us immediate feedback as to what's working and what needs more of our time and attention before it is ready to be released.

Embrace that fact and carry it with you as you pay it forward. Share your epiphanies and actions with me and with others who are interested in coming aboard to feel what it's like to be a part of a caring community.

Please join me on this journey and be open to changing your own life in ways you cannot yet imagine.

Acknowledgements

Education is what remains after one has forgotten what one has learned in school.
~ Albert Einstein

None of us are alone in our life's journey, and there are several people I would like to thank and acknowledge for helping me to move from where I was in 2006 to where I am today. These individuals have provided me with the real life continuing education that makes the difference between surviving and thriving when it comes to online marketing and entrepreneurship.

My very first mentor, before I even understood the true meaning of that word was Raymond Aaron. We met in the spring of 2005 at a real estate event in Los Angeles. He was speaking and I sat down to listen. I have been listening ever since and following his advice and recommendations as to how I may improve and change my life. Our paths continue to cross at locations around the world. There is no such thing as coincidence, and my ongoing friendship with Raymond has proved that out time and again.

When Raymond first asked my opinion on something related to online marketing I knew we had come full circle. Our roles of teacher and student are now interchangeable. I also continue to use his Monthly Mentor™ program to guide my thinking and actions on a daily basis.

The first person to affect my beliefs deeply when it came to online marketing was Marlon Sanders. He was already a legend by then, having come online in the mid 1990s and figuring out things in a way that no one else could have at that point in time.

I don't even remember how I got on to his list, but once I did I was like a hungry child, anxious to gobble up anything and everything he had to offer. I am blessed to now call this man my friend. On a regular basis Marlon makes himself available to speak on the phone with me, and this is where he has shared some of his best ideas and strategies as to how I can continue to grow my business. Being generous with your time and knowledge is a trait that I respect deeply.

During the fall of 2007 I became an affiliate for a course called Teleseminar Secrets. It was created by Alex Mandossian and I had been able to jump start my business as a result of what I learned in that program.

What got Alex's attention was the fact that I had tied for number ten in his affiliate contest with a list of less than a thousand people. This was quite a feat and he wanted to know more about me and what I was doing in my new online business. He scheduled a call with me to discuss this.

Alex and I became fast friends and have now shared the stage at a variety of live events and workshops all over the country. I continue to trust him to share his strategies with me and to recommend what I can do to continue to improve my business.

Within a year I attended my first live event, and it was there that I met Dr. Jeanette Cates. She was also a legend, and I had heard about her being the 'technology tamer'. Because the technical part of this business was already taking its toll on me, I was intrigued by someone who was able to simplify this aspect of the business.

I went up to where she was sitting and introduced myself. She smiled widely and made me feel comfortable. We stayed in touch and within a few months found ourselves at another live event together. I had the audacity to ask her if she would like to teach an online class with me - and she said yes! We went on to teach several online classes and five live events over the next few years and remain good friends to this day.

David Perdew and I were introduced through mutual online friends, and in the spring of 2010 he invited me to co-host a webinar where we would discuss business success principles based on our combined experiences over the years. This led to an invitation to be an instructor and faculty member at his twice annual NAMS (Novice to Advanced Marketing Systems) workshop in Atlanta.

Since that time I have presented at all but one of his workshops, spent almost a week at his remote cabin as a part of a Mastermind, and spoken at two other events where David was also presenting. I consider him to be a friend and confidant and love how his creative brain works.

Dennis Becker came into my life in the summer of 2011. One of my mentoring clients had sent out an email recommending his 'Five Bucks a Day' training, and I signed up to receive it. I was immediately impressed by the combination of simplicity and power of what he was teaching and became a follower of all of his training.

Soon after I became a lifetime member of his Earn 1K a Day forum and membership site, and it wasn't too long after that I was actually doing it (earning a thousand dollars or more in a single day).

In 2012 I first spoke at his annual live event, and now I plan my schedule around speaking there every single year. Dennis is a brilliant and caring individual who continues to be a light in my life.

Introduction

The bigger your why, the easier the how.
~ Jim Rohn

I honestly believe that nearly every experience we have in our lives changes us in some way. This may be accomplished by watching a film that moves us and gets us to think in a new way (I most recently experienced this after seeing *A Walk in the Woods*, the true story of two men who decide to hike the Appalachian Trail). It could come after reading a book, taking a trip, or even after having a chance encounter with a stranger where the conversation takes you to a place you never thought was possible (this happened to me just this past year). My life continues to go down this path, and I live in anticipation of new opportunities and experiences every single day.

This book is intended to get you thinking in new ways about the possibilities of life as an online entrepreneur. Instead of having to navigate these waters alone, I have created a blueprint that is based on my own experiences over the past nine years, as well as those of my students over the past five years. These strategies work!

I have broken down each step of the process of the Trifecta into easy to understand pieces. Together they form a puzzle that is complete and effective.

In the first section I discuss the concept of *Book. Blog. Broadcast.* and why it is such an excellent way to get started quickly. I share how to achieve the level of credibility and visibility that will catapult you to success in a way that makes sense for what you wish to achieve.

Section 2 is about your Mission, your Vision, and your Message, and how your end goals will dictate your actions to a large extent. Then I go into my strategies for maximum productivity in a world where we are constantly interrupted and disrupted from our thoughts. I continue with specific discussions on each of the three prongs, using my own experiences as an example of how to get your plates spinning in a meaningful and useful way to meet your needs.

In the third section I talk about thinking big and setting yourself apart from others by making a name for yourself. You may just find this to be the most worthwhile section of the book when it comes to getting your thinking and mindset into position for greatness in your own life.

The fourth section is where I go into great detail as to exactly how you set up and connect your Trifecta. Without getting too technical I share my specific resources, again based on my personal experiences, so that you will not waste any time, effort, or money putting everything into place.

The final section is a discussion of what can be next in your life as an online entrepreneur. I share how you may wish to teach your topic, become a public speaker and presenter, and going mainstream with your business. This requires you to move way out of your comfort zone and I discuss the best strategies for taking action in this way as well.

You can expect to be taken on a deep dive throughout this book as you explore your options and learn new ways of doing things on the Internet. My wish for you is to take you from where you are today to closer to where you want to be over the next few weeks.

Entrepreneurship is a worthy goal and a path that can lead to a new life for yourself and for your family. Embrace the concepts and ideas I am sharing here with zest and gusto and allow your mind to be open to new possibilities. You can do this!

Section I

Why Is It So Important to Have a Book, a Blog, and a Broadcast?

Chapter 1
Building Credibility and Visibility

Every action or perceived inaction
shapes credibility.
~ Mindy Hall

Is this day and age of content and media overload, we as entrepreneurs must set ourselves apart and make a name for ourselves if we are to rise above the fray and achieve the success we so deserve. As a result of working exclusively online since 2006, I have finally developed a strategy that will allow you to do this in the quickest amount of time possible. It all begins with building credibility and visibility in a way that effectively catapults you to the top of your field as a respected authority on your topic. This is done by simultaneously using my Trifecta of entrepreneurial success: the book, the blog, and the broadcast.

By taking the time and making the effort to write and publish a book on your topic, to blog consistently on this same topic, and to create audios and videos to be published on a variety of media outlets, you will be doing what more than ninety percent of all small business owners and entrepreneurs are not willing to do. This is to write your own ticket when it comes to building credibility and visibility for yourself and for the message you wish to send out into the marketplace. This enables you to reach the most potential prospects and clients at any given time, and to share your knowledge and expertise in a way that few can do by using the three learning modalities of visual, auditory, and tactile sensation.

It wasn't this way during my first several years working online. I got started back in 2006, when writing and publishing a book was still a challenge. You had to get the attention of an agent and a "traditional" publishing house if you wanted to become an author, or you had to spend thousands of dollars with a "vanity" publisher. These were publishers who would print just about anything you wrote, and then charge you a fee for doing so, as well as requiring you to order anywhere from five to ten thousand copies of your book. This truckload of books would be delivered to your front door, where you would carefully stack the boxes in the closet of a spare bedroom or in the garage until you could figure out how to sell them or to give them away.

Blogging was in its infancy, and people would keep online journals that would satisfy their desire to share personal information with the world. It wasn't unusual to find blogs filled with pictures from family reunions or detailed accounts of a vacation or a wedding or other personal event. Teachers began to post lesson plans and other information for excited students and anxious parents using this new medium, and these blogs were indexed by the search engines for everyone to find and read.

Broadcasting via YouTube and iTunes was also in its initial stages, with very few people understanding enough about this new technology to make any headway with using this as an effective marketing tool.

All of this has changed dramatically over the past few years, and we are now at the point where authorship is a dream easily fulfilled, blogging has gone mainstream when it comes to sharing knowledge and expertise with the masses, and broadcasting can be set up quickly and easily to create videos and audios that can be viewed and/or heard live or in replay all over the world. Credibility and visibility becomes your reality when you jump in with this technology and share your message with the world. It is indeed a grand time to be alive as an online entrepreneur.

When you are just getting started with the dream of building an online business, whether your goal is to leave your current job, to just earn some additional income, or to reinvent your life and build an online empire, the strategies that I am sharing in this book will allow you to get there in the shortest span of time.

If this all sounds like a monumental task, rest assured that it is doable. One step at a time, all of which I have outlined in great detail within this book, is how you will be able to build your business as something you will be proud of for a lifetime. As I continue to say to my students, "If I can do it, you can do it, too."

Imagine having clients flock to you and tell you that they see you "everywhere". When you are both visible and credible this is exactly what happens. Becoming attractive to the people who will most benefit from what you have to offer is the promise of what I will be sharing with you.

This all goes back to the "know, like, and trust" factor, where, all things being equal, we prefer to do business with the people we know, like, and trust. Think about how this shapes your own decisions in your daily life to fully understand the power of this concept.

I am often asked how social media comes into play with building credibility and visibility with your book, your blog, and your broadcasts. The simple answer is that it moves seamlessly within your business over time. When people find out about me, sometimes they can't remember if it was through a tweet, an email, one of my blog posts, a podcast, a video, an interview, one of my books, or something else entirely. Meeting me in person is still just a tiny percentage of how people connect with me, and that's due to the influence of social media in all of our lives. I'll be going into much greater detail later on in the book on this topic.

What Do You Want to Be Known For?

Whether we think about this on a conscious level or not, we are all known for something. I believe it's best to make every effort to be known for something of your choosing and design rather than for something conjured up by people who do not even know you on a personal level. Allow me to share some examples of this.

My aunt was a gregarious woman who lit up the room every time she appeared. The problem was that she tended to always make her appearance at the very last moment, long after those who wanted to see her were expecting to spend time with her. Yes, she was habitually late, and that became who she was and what she was known for, instead of the bright shining light that was her true self.

I have another friend who is a brilliant and creative writer and performer. I saw him in a supporting role in a Broadway show where his portrayal of a man living with Multiple Sclerosis brought us all to tears. His traits, talents, and attributes are overshadowed by the fact that he takes almost no pride in his appearance. Yes, he is a slob, and his slovenly manner puts people off long before they spend enough time with him to get to know who he truly is as a human being.

Remember that you are the brand of your online business as an entrepreneur. It is you people wish to connect with, and you want your reputation to precede you so that others can find you and become your raving fans. Remember that first impressions are lasting ones and make every effort to put your best foot forward at all times. Resist the urge to believe the argument that you must be allowed to "be yourself" and that others will just have to accept you for who you are. That may work with your family and close acquaintances, but in business it carries no weight. The world of online business is your oyster when you show your best side consistently and work to have credibility and visibility in your back pocket at all times and in all circumstances.

Be willing and determined to lay this foundation from the very beginning and I promise you that your business will flourish. Do this slowly and carefully at first, allowing yourself to first find your voice and get into the rhythm of creating content that will represent you well for years to come. What we publish to the internet stays there for eternity, so make it your goal to put your best foot forward from the very beginning.

Those who do not heed my advice often find themselves living their first year of entrepreneurship over and over again, until one day they finally come to the conclusion that these concepts work, and work well, as they establish themselves as an authority on their topic and an expert in their niche.

And those who take action and move forward with determination and intent will find themselves at the center of discussion on their topic, an enviable place to be in when it comes to building credibility and visibility for your business.

In the next chapter I will discuss this three pronged approach to the concept of book, blog, broadcast and why it is so important in the world we live in today.

Chapter 2
The Concept of Book, Blog, and Broadcast

*Look up at the stars and not down at your feet. Try to
make sense about what you see, and wonder about
what makes the universe exist. Be curious.*
~ Stephen Hawking

I came upon the concept of book, blog, broadcast purely
by accident, even though I firmly believe there are no
accidents or coincidences in the universe. Because I was a
new entrepreneur and due to the fact that we are still in the
pioneering stages of working online, it took me several years
to figure out that three dimensional is much better than one
dimensional in all cases when growing a business and the
relationships that come along with it.

It is my honest opinion that there is no better voice than
the one that comes from experience. Listening to that voice
and tailoring your actions to what you learn from it is a whole
different matter. With that said I will share my experiences
with you in the areas of authorship, blogging, and
broadcasting in a way that will shed light on how you can use
this strategy to build your own lucrative and successful
business in the shortest time possible. It's an example of the
principle that having a plan, getting to work, and following

through makes all of the difference when it comes to getting our message out to the world.

First, I must share with you that I was not a writer until I started my business on the internet in 2006. Until that time I was someone who talked regularly about writing, but did very little of it. Even though I took creative writing classes, and classes on poetry, screenwriting, and other genres, putting pen to paper or fingers to keyboard was not my strong suit. Instead, I would share my ideas and stories out loud with others, leaving them as thought clouds that would never manifest into actual written form. I was filled with good intentions that never came to fruition. This cost me dearly as one opportunity after another passed me by over the years due to my inaction and inability to follow through with my dreams.

This all changed when I came online. I saw almost immediately that writing would be the fastest way for me to get the word out about whom I was and what I was doing as an entrepreneur. That's when I began blogging and writing articles, and it was a painful process until I got into the habit of writing every single day. I would start with a list of three ideas or concepts I wanted to share within my article or blog post and then write a few sentences about each one. I developed something I called the "5 Paragraph Model™" that I continue to teach to my students as they begin the entrepreneurial journey through their writing.

In the spring of 2007 I challenged myself to write one hundred articles within one hundred days. That did not happen...I wrote all of them during the first seventy-eight days!

By forcing myself to sit down in front of the computer and write three hundred word articles each day I turned myself into a writer. I have now written well over two thousand blog posts, several thousand articles, more than ten thousand email messages to my lists, and twelve full length books. This amounts to more than half a million words, something this is still difficult for me to fathom. For someone who didn't write much at all before starting my online business, I continue to make up for that in a huge way these days.

The point I am making here is that you can do the exact same thing. It's all done one idea, one sentence, one paragraph, one article, one blog post, one chapter at a time.

The concept of broadcasting is one that I didn't fully embrace until around 2010. Up until then I was focused on creating written content exclusively. Once the bright light came on in my mind's eye about the power of combining the written word with the spoken word and the visual world, the idea came together for what would become the book, blog, broadcast phenomena.

I teach that allowing someone to hear your voice or see and hear you in a video is the next best thing to meeting them in person. It's a virtual hug and handshake that bridges the gap between the dimensions. They are immediately drawn to your voice and to your image and can either resonate with your message or move on to someone else. This is a powerful concept that so many online entrepreneurs fail to understand.

Here is a living example of what I mean by this: I challenge you to go to your email inbox right now and scroll through your emails from the past day or two. As you click on each one, think about who it is from and how you are connected with them. If it is from someone you know personally, can you hear and see them in your mind's eye? What about the emails you receive from marketers and other business people; have you ever met them in person, seen them in a video, or heard them in an audio recording? If so, then are you able to visualize their face, or hear the tone of their voice while you are reading their email message? Now, read through an email from someone you have never met in person or heard on an audio. What is that experience like? It will most likely be one dimensional, where you feel little or no connection with the person who is writing. Be willing to flesh yourself out as a three-dimensional being with the help of audio and video in your business.

Blogging

My first experience with blogging goes back to the early 2000s, while I was still working as a classroom teacher. There was a platform available from Google called Blogger, where you could keep a written online journal and publish it to the World Wide Web, as the internet was referred to in its early stages. A blog was known as a "web log" and people everywhere began setting them up and sharing their innermost thoughts and knowledge on an array of topics.

The history of this is quite interesting, and I'll share a bit of it here with you. In 1999 Blogger was actually launched by a company called Pyra Labs. Pyra's founder, Evan Williams, was an employee at Google at that time. It was the earliest online, dedicated publishing tools, and it was a paid platform. Google acquired them in 2003 and turned this service into the largest one of its kind within the next year. They purchased a service called Picasa, and then integrated Picasa and its photo sharing utility *Hello* into Blogger, allowing users to post photos to their blogs. In 2004 Blogger introduced a major redesign, adding features such as web standards-compliant templates, individual archive pages for posts, comments, and posting by email. This migrated all current users to Google servers (called BlogSpot) and had some new features, including interface language in French, Italian, German and Spanish.

I started one of these web logs on the topic of science, and quickly shared it with my students. This technology, although quite user friendly, had many features that were confusing and ambiguous. One day as I added yet another science lesson idea to my blog I ventured over to the user interface and began clicking around to see what I could find.

Remember that I just mentioned a feature that allowed you to change the language of your web log into French, Spanish, Italian, or German? I changed mine into German, a language I know fewer than ten words of, and continued to investigate. I clicked here and there and then my screen went blank. Everything was deleted, gone forever, and never to be retrieved from the depths of cyberspace. I learned later that I had inadvertently clicked on the word *cancellare*, which in German means to delete. I had deleted several months of work, and I had learned my lesson.

When I came online I refused to go back to Blogger, and ended up on a platform called Typepad. This was a paid service that hosted your blogs and allowed you to easily publish your posts to the world. During my first year, between 2006 and 2007, I had about a dozen blogs. Every day I worked feverishly to maintain them with fresh content, only to learn that I was spreading myself way too thin to get any leverage. I had blogs on a variety of topics, including one where I wrote about my dogs (my "Dog Blog"), one on healthy eating and exercise, one on real estate, and even one on the Law of Attraction, to name just a few of them. I finally came to the realization that I needed to focus on just one area if I were to become successful. I chose my blog on helping others to write and market an eBook on their niche topic, and my site at eBookWritingandMarketingSecrets.com was born. These days that particular domain is forwarded to my site at ConnieRagenGreen.com so that people who knew of me years ago can still find me at my new home.

In 2008 WordPress became much more user friendly, and droves of people doing business online switched their sites over to this platform. I had a web master do this for me so that I could move forward with technology more easily. Having a hosted site allows you to own and control your blog, something that cannot be done on free sites and even those paid sites that maintain at least some control over what you publish and how you run your business.

At this point in time I began mentoring others, and blogging became my marketing choice for all of us to make a name for ourselves online. That's when I began referring to a blog as your "home on the internet", a phrase I coined and continue to teach today.

Blogging at least twice a week during your first year and two or three times each month thereafter is still the very best strategy.

Authorship

I chose to discuss blogging first as a way to lead into the concept of authorship. This was done in order to show the power of posting regularly to a blog as a way to alleviate the pain and suffering of jumping into the task of writing a full length book, especially if you are not already in the habit of writing on a daily basis.

It had been my dream to publish a book since I was about twelve years old. It was my mother who first put this idea into my head, and I can remember daydreaming about putting my stories into print. Some days I would "think" out complete story lines, filled with characters, setting, and a plot, only to let it all disappear into the recesses of my mind because I did not write any of it down. Occasionally I would write a poem or a short story, but that was usually related to a class assignment where I needed to actually produce some work. I was not disciplined enough to complete any writing on my own, save for the random Mother's Day poem or short essay for another relative or adult friend of the family.

When I came online in 2006 I quickly realized that writing needed to be a part of my day, every day, if I were to build and grow the type of business I was dreaming of. As the years went by my dream of writing and publishing a book grew stronger, but I still didn't know how it was all going to come together for me. Three people came into my life who helped me to change both my mindset and my strategy on how this was going to transpire.

The first person was Raymond Aaron, the man I consider to be my very first mentor. Raymond and I had met at a real estate conference in Los Angeles during the spring of 2005. At that time I was still teaching school full time and working in real estate after school, weekends, and during my vacation time. When I heard him speak on the topic of 'Living a Mentored Life' I immediately resonated with the message he was sharing and signed up for his Monthly Mentor™ program. Within a few short months I made the decision to resign from the school district by the end of the following year, to give away my current real estate clients, and to start my own business online that I could run from home, or from wherever in the world I happened to be at the time.

Raymond and I became friends over time, and I would attend any events where he was speaking if at all possible. My online business began to grow, and coincidentally, we both ended up in Atlanta to speak at an event hosted by marketer Matt Bacak in the fall 2007. Matt was shocked to find out that we knew each other, because he had just met Raymond on the plane as they were both returning from a speaking engagement in Australia.

At the end of my presentation that day in Atlanta, Raymond insisted that we go out for lunch to talk about it. I could tell from the tone of his voice that he was not pleased, and we proceeded to have a discussion I will never forget. He explained what I had done right (very little, in his opinion) and what could, and should be changed. I took copious notes that day and the result was that I prepared a completely new presentation on how to make huge profits with a tiny list. I trusted him and his opinions meant the world to me. I never thought of him as being unkind in his abrupt and direct approach with me that day; instead, I took his constructive criticism as coming from someone who truly cares about me and my success.

Almost simultaneously, I was connecting with Alex Mandossian as he taught his "Teleseminar Secrets" course. I got Alex's attention by becoming one of his top affiliates while my list was still quite small, with fewer than a thousand names in my database at that time. When we had a phone consultation he told me I'd be perfect as the "huge profits, tiny list" person and that I should start a blog on this topic. I mentioned Alex earlier in this book when I acknowledged him for helping me to shape my life and my business.

After hearing almost the same idea from two top people in my field, I sat up and took notice and got to work. I committed to blogging twice a week on this topic of how to use relationship marketing to increase your income if you are new to online entrepreneurship and only have a tiny list. But even though I was doing this, the bright light didn't turn on for me until I met a third person who would become pivotal in my entrepreneurial journey.

This person was Jeanette Cates, and I met her in 2008 while at a conference in Atlanta. She was already a legend in the online world, having been a part of since the mid 1990s. I was honored to connect with her and we became fast friends.

Soon we were teaching online courses together and even co-hosted five live events, known as the Online Revenue Workshops, over the next several years. But it was a conversation we had in Las Vegas during the fall of 2009 that changed everything for me. I also acknowledged Jeanette in the beginning of this book.

I had brought up the subject of wanting to write a book, and said that I couldn't possible take three or four months away from my online business in order to make that happen.

Jeanette looked me straight in the eye and said something I will never forget:

"Why on earth would you need to do that? Just write for one hour each day, and repurpose your blog posts on your topic to create the content."

I'm not exactly sure what transpired next, but I believe my mouth fell open and I was unable to speak for a least a couple of minutes. Jeanette had the answer I was looking for, and I "blogged my book" over the next three months by writing for about one hour each day.

The result was *Huge Profits With a Tiny List: 50 Ways to Use Relationship Marketing to Increase Your Bottom Line*. It was published in the summer of 2010 and became the first of many books that would catapult me to success as a bestselling author. The concept of connecting a blog with a book was born in my mind, even though it would take another couple of years to flesh it out into what would become the strategies I am teaching you here.

Broadcasting

The idea of hosting your own radio or television show with a few mouse clicks is still a miracle in my mind. And the ability to "live stream" to the world through platforms like Periscope and Meercat is an amazing feat of technology. We are indeed fortunate to be living during this time. Blab is the latest player in this arena, and I haven't taken the time to see how it differs from other platforms. I would encourage you to experiment for yourself and see what you discover, in terms of how it would benefit your entrepreneurial endeavors.

If I can give you any advice on this at all it would be to keep everything you do short and to the point. Write down a few key points you would like to cover during your broadcast and then cover them. Also, be sure to say your name and website at the beginning and at the end of what you record.

I will be going into much greater detail on this topic later on in the book, so for now just be open to learning as much as you can and them implementing what you have learned so you can see the immediate results of your actions.

Driving Traffic

Incorporating all three of these strategies – writing a book, maintaining a blog, and broadcasting your information – will allow you to drive traffic from every major source available, including Amazon, Bing, Yahoo!, Google, iTunes, and YouTube, as well as from social media sites such as Twitter, Facebook, LinkedIn, and Pinterest. Your specific keywords will open the door to your prospects finding you quickly and easily, sometimes within minutes of beginning their search.

Try this out for yourself to see what I mean. Start with Google and type something into the search box. The example I will use is that of "writing good headlines". I did this search recently to help a client find out who was writing about this topic as a way to connect with these authorities, connect with them through their blogs, books, and podcasts, and to find one or two blog posts to curate (more on this topic later on) for her own blog.

Just on page one the search results included blog posts from Jeff Goins, Neil Patel, Brian Clark and his team at CopyBlogger, and Dan Poynter. These people are all authorities and experts in this area and on this topic, and their sites contain a wealth of information. I advised my client to follow each of these people on their blogs and on social media, and to begin posting to her own blog in a way that shows off her own expertise and understanding of copywriting.

The search results also included Google Plus postings from social media maven Mari Smith and Nick Usborne, a fill-in-the-blanks lesson on writing effective headlines from the University of Kansas, a featured article from HubSpot that included an infographic that could easily be pinned on Pinterest (more on this later one), an informative article from WordStream, and a curated post from the CoSchedule blog.

Within one minute I had all of this research right in front of me, and I explained to my client how these results would give her enough information and ideas to lay the foundation and build her business over the next thirty days.

Do this same thing by Googling the phrases you want to be found for and then researching the people and sites that are returned as the results. Make it your goal and intention to connect with these others to learn from them and to share your own thoughts and ideas on the topics you are already knowledgeable about. Commenting on their blogs, adding your opinions and ideas on social media, and purchasing their books and other trainings will move you closer to the inner circle of influence and allow you to also make a name for yourself. I have watched numerous people do this since coming online in 2006, and you would be amazed at the big names that got their start in this way.

And before I forget to mention this, be sure to do a regular Google search for your own name to see what comes back. Be sure to use parentheses around your name (mine would be "connie ragen green") so that you will only find results where your entire name is used. I like to print out the first two pages every month or so to see how it changes over time. Your social media connections will most likely appear near the top of page one, and hopefully your main blog(s) and websites will follow close behind.

Getting your own message out to the world has never been easier, and you have it all right in front of you when you are connected to the Internet. People want and need to know who you are and what you have to say, in a way that only you can say it. We have all had the experience of hearing something over and over and over again, only to finally take action when someone says it in a way that resonates with us. Can you relate to what I am saying here?

In this world of information, it is completely up to us to utilize this information in a way that will effectively move us forward in a direction that makes sense and feels right at our very core. Driving targeted traffic to our own sites simply becomes a matter of finding where the traffic is right now and standing in front of it to get our share. The internet is amazing!

Show Me The Money!

At this point you may be thinking that this all sounds well and good, but wondering how you can turn this into a profitable business. That's the right question to be asking yourself at this point, and rest assured that I will answer it in full throughout the remainder of this book as I explain the different business models available to us an online entrepreneurs.

For now, think about the fact that no one earns income without someone purchasing something from you or from someone else, and that having a variety of products and services for sale is crucial. Start with the question "What's for sale?" to see where you are right now.

I began with affiliate marketing, meaning that I did not have any of my own products and services during my first year online. Instead, I recommended other people's products and services in return for a commission. Early on I established myself and built a reputation as someone who would only recommend what I purchased, used, and benefitted from, and this allowed me to begin earning some income on a regular basis. At the end of the first year I released my first information product. It was a four week online course, and when it was over I offered it as a home study course. It sold for a hundred dollars as a live training and a hundred fifty dollars afterwards. This became a model I used time and again over the next three years as I continued to learn more about being an online entrepreneur.

Next, I began marketing for small business owners. This was an excellent way for me to earn some income while I was building my primary, or core, business. I described it to my prospects as helping them to "make the phone ring". I brought all of the knowledge and information I was gathering into a strategy that enabled me to "earn while I learned". I was completely honest with the people I helped, and they enjoyed being a part of the journey. My enthusiasm made up for my lack of experience, and soon they were getting new clients for their business.

It's funny, but at the time I didn't even count this income as a part of what I was doing online. Somehow, in my mind I discounted small business marketing as a viable income stream and it wasn't until about two years later when I realized that earning five to seven thousand dollars a month for setting up blogs, writing, and marketing in this way was such an important part of the overall process of building my online business.

Creating information products came next, and I have already shared that I was a full year into my business and already increasing my income steadily each month before I released my first one of these. I can now come up with an idea, create the product, write the sales letter, and release it within just a few days. You'll be able to do the same as soon as you get some practice and experience in doing so under your belt.

Next I began creating membership sites, which are simply virtual versions of groups connected through common interests and goals. You may wish to begin with a free level of membership, and then add a paid level as you gain more confidence and have more content to share with your members. I recommend always including a live component to what you offer so that people can feel that direct connection with you.

Niche site marketing involves setting up a site on a niche topic, perhaps one that is of interest or already familiar to you and creating relevant content to attract people who are also interested in learning more. You can then either recommend books and products as an affiliate, or even create your own to sell on and through your niche site. I love niche sites as an additional method of "learning while you earn" on the internet.

Coaching and mentoring are also excellent business models, but I will caution you to think long and hard about how this will work for you. I find that working closely with more than twenty people in any given year saps my energy and detracts from my ability to help them in the way I wish to while they are coming to me for guidance.

I never schedule more than two calls on any given day, as that enables me to better serve the needs of my clients. Also, make sure that the people you take on as clients resonate with your own values and belief system. Twice I have agreed to work with people who did not fit well into my groups, and everyone suffered as a result.

Consulting with small businesses, as well as with corporations and non-profits, continues to be one of my favorite business models. This work tends to come after you have made a name for yourself, so get started right away if you think this is a direction you would like to pursue in the future.

Section II

What Is the Entrepreneurial Trifecta of Writing a Book, Maintaining a Blog, and Developing a Podcast?

Chapter 3
What Is Your Vision?

Most men lead lives of quiet desperation and go to the
grave with the song still in them.
~ Henry David Thoreau

As you begin to create your business in the way that I am explaining and outlining in this book, you must decide where it is that you wish to go with it over time. Envision your life in one year, in five years, and even further out if you possibly can. It wasn't until I made the decision back in 2004 to leave my job as a classroom teacher that I fully understood the power of projecting your vision into the future and then 'reverse engineering' your way from where you are right now to closer to where you would like to be at some point in the future.

If you are not familiar with this term, 'reverse engineering' in the technical world is the process of taking apart an object to see how it works in order to duplicate or enhance the object. The practice, taken from older industries, is now frequently used on computer hardware and software.

In the context I am using it here, reverse engineering is the mental process of visualizing yourself in the near and not too far future in an effort to see what steps and actions you must take in order to achieve the goals you have set out for yourself. I have used this successfully with my health and weight loss, as well as with books I have written, courses I have taught, and live events I have hosted. By having an end goal in mind, or at least in my mind's eye from the first day I can simply rewind the movie to see what comes next.

What Is Your End Goal?

Depending upon what stage of your life you are currently living, your end goal will vary. For me, I think of my life as being almost ideal at this time. I have the time and financial freedom to live how and where I please, and to be involved with the people and the activities that bring me the greatest joy and satisfaction.

The thought of retiring is not one I can relate to at all, as my business is one that can go on indefinitely for many years to come. Even as the technology changes and the marketplace shifts, I will be able to roll with the tide and even make a few waves of my own. It is a desirable position to be in and I am grateful every single moment for what I have been able to create for myself and my loved ones.

You may or may not resonate with what I have just shared. Perhaps the end goal you have in mind is to use your online business as a stepping stone to something else entirely. You may have adult children you would like to help, or to bring into your business alongside of you. You may dream of starting a brick and mortar or other type of business later on. Or, you may wish to earn enough income from what I am teaching here to retire to an island in the middle of the ocean. The only thing that matters is that you have a clear idea of where you want to be at some point in the future.

Your Mission and Vision

When I wrote earlier about getting your message out to the world, I was referring to your Mission and your Vision. I think of a Mission as being the day to day tasks and activities that will allow you to carry out your Vision during this lifetime. My Mission is to find and work with the people who have an entrepreneurial spirit and calling and help them to succeed with their own businesses by teaching them the steps to take and the actions that will enable them to achieve their goals.

My Vision, on the other hand, is to empower men and women around the world to reach their highest potential by boldly moving forward towards their dreams.

You can see that these two perspectives share some overlap, but that the former speaks more to the actions I will take on a daily basis while the latter is more about my big dreams for a lifetime.

Please heed my advice with this: dare to dream big, big, big! As my friend Joe Vitale puts it, *aude aliquid dignum*. This is from sixteenth century Latin and translates to mean 'dare something worthy'. When I made the conscious decision to leave my life as a classroom teacher and a real estate broker and residential appraiser behind and seek a new life as an entrepreneur, I was daring to begin something worthy. You can do this in your own life as well and live as you have never before even imagined.

I began this chapter with the well known quote from Henry David Thoreau:

> *Most men lead lives of quiet desperation and go to the grave with the song still in them.*

I implore you to do everything in your power to prevent this from describing your life, even for a single day. Instead, create a vision for your life and business. Write it down now, before you forget, and know that it will grow and evolve over time into one that fits your lifestyle and the dreams you have for what you wish to achieve during this lifetime. Remember that this is not an audition; we are actually living the life God gave us and that every moment is a precious one to be nurtured and cherished.

For years I have known and see examples of the idea that our thoughts are indeed things, and living your best life will get you closer to where you want to be much more quickly than simply living a life where contentment is your goal. Think about what you want and then go after it. Life is much too short to do otherwise.

Share Your Message

In the very beginning you may not think of yourself as someone who has a message they feel must be shared with the world. I felt that way and thought I was simply creating a business that would enable me to work from home and still earn enough to pay all of my bills.

Over time I came to realize that I did have a message I needed to send in a loud and clear way. The message was that anyone can become an online entrepreneur and change their life forever. Now I shout that message from both the virtual and the physical rooftops any time I have the opportunity to share what I do each day with other people.

Turn your message into one that can be a tag line for your blog, a part of your brand, and a catchy phrase to include at the end of your emails and as your signature line. Soon, people will come to associate you with this, and you will fill the shoes you have set out for yourself.

It all comes down to sharing who you really are with the world. Do not be afraid to show vulnerability and to open up to your prospects and clients as you build your business.

As a result of my message that anyone who wants to can become an entrepreneur, my connections with charities and non-profits continues to grow. I love making loans to entrepreneurs in Third World and developing countries through the KIVA program. I work with high school students through Rotary's Interact program. And I mentor local people of all ages as they find their way to the life they want and deserve.

Let your message become your mantra. Repeat it over and over to anyone who will listen. Write about it. Be open to honest discussions about it so that you can see other perspectives and refine your own belief system. This single process will bring you growth of untold proportions over the coming years.

Chapter 4
Writing and Publishing a Book

If there's a book that you want to read, but it hasn't been written yet, then you must write it.
~ Toni Morrison

Please remember that when I discuss the idea of writing your book, I am referring to a *full length, non-fiction book.* Fiction is a very different genre and one that does not fit at all into the business model I am teaching here.

By full-length I mean a book of between twenty-five and forty thousand words, published in paperback in the six by nine inch format, and containing anywhere from one hundred twenty to one hundred sixty pages. Anything smaller than this I consider to be a 'pamphlet' and anything larger is simply too unwieldy to serve your needs. This book came in at just over thirty-three thousand words, if that helps to put this all in perspective.

I publish everything on Amazon through what is known as their Create Space program first. Create Space is Amazon's Print on Demand publishing division and this program changed the face of book publishing over the past six years or so. It put the power into the hands of the authors and readers as to what would be published and read on any given topic. It isn't a perfect system and solution, but most of us, myself included, would not be bestselling published authors it if had not been for this.

The site is self-explanatory, and you only need a PDF (portable document format) version of your book, available with Microsoft Word, Open Office, and most other word processing program to begin. You'll also need a cover design and an ISBN (International Standard Book Number) and then you're ready to publish in paperback format.

Later on you will release your book for Kindle. That's a simple process as well, but there are a few requirements and restrictions that are clearly explained on Amazon's site.

It may seem like I am oversimplifying the process here, but the truth is that Amazon has made it extremely easy for anyone to become a published author without having to jump through the hoops that continue to be the standard for more traditional publishers.

One step that I took early on was to form my own publishing company with Geoff Hoff, a man I continue to respect and admire as an author, entrepreneur, and self-made man. Our company is Hunter's Moon Publishing and we pride ourselves on only publishing the highest quality manuscripts for a select group of people. Through our publishing house we own a block of ISBNs that set us apart from the majority of people who publish through Amazon's Create Space program. I highly recommend you do the same, and feel free to get in touch with either Geoff or myself if you need more assistance with this process.

Do not be intimidated by this process. You will have moments of doubt and feelings of inadequacy throughout the process. Stand firm in knowing that you indeed have something value to say and that no one can deliver your message in the way that you can and will. Have no fear that your final product will be a blessing in the hands of those who want and need the information and experiences you are sharing.

Researching Your Topic

I like to use Amazon as a resource for researching my topic before I write a book. This site provides a wealth of knowledge and information you will find helpful. Search for the 'Players' and the 'Movers and Shakers' in your field to see what they've already written. If you are not sure who these people are, then go over to Google and spend some time to find them.

Next, do a search for books on your general topic to see what's already available. And remember, the goal is not to write a book on a topic that has never been written about; instead, your goal is to corner one specific aspect of your market and to become the person best known for it. Can you see the difference?

You also want to know what the accepted philosophy is on your topic. That will help set you apart when you enter the picture with your own unique perspective. No one will see your topic in exactly the same way that you do because no one will have had even similar life experiences.

If you've read any of these, leave a detailed review. This will also build your credibility over time. Make it a point to read every book written on your topic and you will be light years ahead of everyone else.

Do a 'Look Inside' to see what the books are about. This feature makes it simple to get new ideas and to find keywords that you may never have thought of.

Once you have found authors who write on your topic join their lists, read their blogs, and connect with them on the various social media sites. Find out what's for sale in their funnel. This may take extra time and effort but it will be worth it as you build your online business.

Later on I will be explaining exactly how you will take the ideas in your head and get them down into written matter that will become your book. For now, explore the ideas whirling around in your mind and make some notes about what you would most like to discuss in the book. Knowing that the process has never been easier and simpler will be reassurance that you can achieve your goal of becoming a published author as a part of this three-pronged approach to entrepreneurial success.

Chapter 5
Your Blog

The best and most beautiful things in the world cannot be
seen or even touched - they must be felt with the heart.
~Helen Keller

I have already stated that your blog is your "home on the Internet" and serves as a venue in which you can find your voice and share your ideas, knowledge, and expertise on your topic with others. Later on in Chapter 10, I will tell you more about actually setting up your site, but here is where I want to explain more about how your blog will serve you for years to come as you build your online business and embrace the idea of entrepreneurship for the rest of your life.

Use your blog as a sounding board for your thoughts and ideas on a variety of topics. And remember that because you own and control your site, your goal is to bring people from sites like Facebook and Twitter back to your site to read your posts and to comment on them. I so often see people sharing the link to one of their posts on social media, only to spur an active discussion on the topic. Within a day or two that thread is pushed further down the page as new posts and updates are added, and the blogger never had the benefit of having that discussion and those comments archived on their own site. Please do not make this mistake. If it begins to happen, ask readers to bring the discussion over to your blog, and then make sure to reply to each and every one of the comments there.

I was truly able to 'find my voice' by blogging, and by this I mean that I got into the habit of writing almost every day during that first year I was online and feeling more comfortable sharing my thoughts, ideas, and opinions in written format. I never would have been able to write my first book, let alone twelve books now, if I hadn't used my blog as the platform to share my words and my message with the world.

Later on I will also go into greater detail about setting up your blog, but for now suffice it to say that you will be using a hosted WordPress site. This means that you will own and control everything you publish here, and the cost is just pennies a day.

Think about this site as the control center for your entire online empire. Your books and your broadcasts will have homes here as well, allowing others to know as much as possible about you and your message. When people Google us our name site tends to come up first, especially if we have optimized it by using our name strategically throughout the blog. This brings them straight over to this site where they can learn all about you and what you have to offer them if they are the right prospects for your topic.

I highly recommend posting to your blog at least twice a week during the first year, once a week during the second year, and at least twice a month thereafter. This builds a solid foundation for everything you are working to build in your online business. You may wish to write two or three posts in one sitting and then schedule them to go out two or three days apart so that the search engines can see that you are posting with some regular frequency.

Also, once you set up your podcast each of those will become an additional post that counts for the numbers I suggested above. I like to write about four hundred words for each podcast post, reiterating what I discussed on the call.

The sidebar is of prime importance as well. At the top, add your free giveaway and optin form. Below that you may want to include a link to your book or books on Amazon, your most recent tweets on Twitter, recent posts and comments, your list of categories, and affiliate offers, all in that order. You can change these within minutes at any time, so do not worry if they are not exactly the way you want them right now.

The key to successful blogging is consistency. I now write every day, and this has allowed me the opportunity to explore my thoughts and ideas in written form, create information products, become a public speaker, and also to improve my writing. Without my own venue for writing on my topic I would be lost at sea when it comes to bringing my thoughts into tangible form and my ideas to fruition.

Chapter 6
Your Broadcast

Start by doing what's necessary;
then do what's possible;
and suddenly you are doing the impossible.
~ Francis of Assisi

Originally I referred to this section and part of my three-pronged entrepreneurial strategy as 'Podcasting', but I soon realized there was so much more we could do when we expanded this idea to one of broadcasting across several platforms simultaneously. During the past five years or so I have created a channel on YouTube where I upload short (less than five minutes is best) videos expressing a simple message, continued to host two popular podcasts, used teleseminars as a way to educate and entertain my prospects and clients, and have also branched out to live streaming as well.

I was the last person in the world anyone would have thought would embrace this type of media and marketing in such a big way, but once I began it became second nature to use these platforms to get my message out to the world. I had always been the person behind the camera and would make every effort not to have my picture taken. Video was not as common, so in the remote chance someone wanted to include me in their video I would quickly decline. Once I came online I saw immediately that this strategy was not going to serve me well, and that I needed to be grateful that others wanted to have their picture taken with me. Once I adopted this 'attitude of gratitude' everything changed. Now I'm always ready for my close up and friends and family continue to tease me about being such a ham.

For now, think about how you would like to be perceived on video and in audio recordings. It took me many months to get used to the sound of my own voice, and now it is music to my ears. I'm still not used to seeing myself in videos, so I take every opportunity to watch the ones I am in and to give myself some constructive criticism along the way. Just a small change, such as combing your hair in a different way or wearing (or not wearing) certain colors makes a huge difference.

Later on I will be going into great detail as to the exact steps you must take in order to be successful at the broadcasting piece of this completely doable puzzle. For now, make some notes, visit iTunes and YouTube and do a keyword search of the phrases most closely related to your topic, and think about how you would like to be perceived when your prospects and clients see and hear you in the near future.

Section III

What If You Write a Book, Blog, and Broadcast?

Chapter 7
Thinking BIG!

Our deepest fear is not that we are inadequate.
Our deepest fear is that we are powerful beyond measure.
~ Marianne Williamson

The absolute worst thing that can occur as you take this journey is for you to develop what I refer to as *the fear of thinking big*. I love the quote above that expresses it so beautifully. My experience so far has been to discover that I am indeed capable of achieving all of my hopes, wishes, and dreams, simply by moving forward each day and taking both inspired and appropriate action towards my goals.

Yes, this can be scary and lonely many times, but once I have pushed through my fears and feelings of inadequacy I have a feeling of pride and accomplishment that I would not trade for anything in the world.

The truth is that we must work daily to get out of our comfort zone. Just about everything we do for the first time is scary, if you stop to think about it. As young children we are fearless. Then as we get a little older we allow others to intimidate us and our confidence is slowly but surely whittled away.

Over the twenty years I worked as a classroom teacher I saw this time and again. The confident and cheerful Kindergartner became a more reserved first grader and by the time that same child came to me as a fifth grader they were self-conscious and sullen. This occurred as a result of so many factors, including peer pressure, academic rigor, and situations where children and adults alike were made to feel like they were not worthy and not enough. It happened to me during my teaching career, so I can only imagine what it was like for my students.

While I was a classroom teacher we had something called 'Three Stars and a Wish'. This was a way for my students to learn how to give others constructive criticism while also learning how to give compliments. It worked like this:

Before you could say something to someone about their academic performance (your wish), you needed to find three positive things to say (your stars). For instance, if someone was not paying attention and always losing their place while we read aloud, you might say something like 'I like how you help pass out the readers so that we can begin our lesson on time; I like how you call everyone by name when you are doing this; and I like how you sit quietly while others are taking their turn reading. I wish that you would follow along so that you would always be at the right place when you are called on to read.'

When you are ten or eleven years old this is not an easy skill to master. But once you did it was as if you held the secret to the universe in your words. Soon this 'three stars and a wish' scenario carried outside of our classroom walls and on to the playground and into the students' homes. It built confidence and gave them powerful tools for dealing with others.

When I got started online I felt like I couldn't do much at all. My own confidence and self-esteem was at an all time low and I believed that I might be destined for mediocrity for the remainder of my days. Can you imagine feeling that way while you are in the prime of your life?

When I made the decision to find a way to change my life, I looked for guidance from anywhere I could find it. My current friends and circle of influence included people that were also just living in "existence mode", so I knew I had to be more creative in my search for something new.

This understanding of my current circumstances set me on a journey that would take me to the far reaches of the planet and connect me with some of the most original thinkers I would ever meet.

A Chance Meeting and a Long Hike

I had a friend named Alicia who heard me talking about wanting to do a different type of work. One night in March of 2005 she invited me out to dinner, where some new friends of hers would also be joining us. They were charming people, and they shared how they had left their jobs in the corporate world in order to have more time with their two children.

In order to continue earning enough income they had taken classes on 'day trading'. This is a way to buy and sell stocks within a very short window of time that I still don't know much about or understand. What impressed me the most was the way they talked about their new life with such enthusiasm and zest for life; a true joie de vivre. I wanted to know more, so we arranged to go on a hike the following Saturday morning. They suggested getting started by five o'clock and I agreed without hesitation.

We chose a place called O'Melveny Park, deep in the Santa Susana Mountains not far from where we all lived at that time. I had hiked there on numerous occasions with the Sierra Club and knew that one of the trails went up to the very top of El Cielo Peak. The summit is more than twenty-five hundred feet to the top, or about eight hundred meters. I had never attempted to hike to the top of this trail, but I'm not sure why that was.

Of course, when my new friends arrived early that morning they began heading up that way and I followed along without saying a word. It was at that moment I realized that in order to change my life I would need to approach situations much differently than I had done in the past.

Over the next four hours we talked about anything and everything and nothing at all. What I mean by this is that I instantly felt like I had known them for years, even though we had just met a few days earlier at dinner. We shared stories, and dreams, and ideas in a way that was unfamiliar with me among my friends and family members. It was clear to me these people had come into my life not by chance or by coincidence, but because of my thoughts and intentions. This may sound very 'out there' but it's exactly how I felt at the time and still feel today, more than ten years later.

I allowed this couple to guide me towards a new way of thinking over the next few months. They suggested books for me to read, CDs for me to listen to, and videos for me to watch. In the beginning it was a tedious process for me to get through another chapter before going to sleep at night or to listen to yet another audio recording on my way to school early in the morning. Once I got into the habit of allowing new information and ideas into my brain each day I began to think differently. I once again had hopes and dreams that I had put on the back burner for so many years; I was thinking BIG!

But I'm getting way ahead of myself here. When one person or event comes into your consciousness, another is soon to follow, and it was during the following month, April of 2005 that the next thing happened to me.

I woke up one morning and felt like my life was about to change. I can't accurately describe this feeling, but I will tell you that it brought a wave of joy and hope over me that I had not experienced ever in the past. I allowed myself to be overcome with the feeling until it finally subsided.

A few hours later I received a call from a friend, asking me to join him the following weekend at a real estate Expo at the convention center in downtown Los Angeles. I said that I could join him on Saturday, but that I had way too much work to do to commit to the entire weekend.

He and I drove downtown early the following Saturday morning, and agreed to stay at least until noon. We split up, each of us exploring different speakers and booths so that we could compare notes later on. I went into the main area and heard one of the keynote speakers, and then I went up and down the aisles where I could heard each speaker's voice as I passed by.

There were presentations on a variety of real estate topics, including short sales, foreclosures, probate sales, and more. Then I heard a voice that didn't seem to be discussing anything about real estate at all.

This man was talking about 'living a mentored life', a concept I was not familiar with. And even before I saw him I could feel his energy and emotion as he went on and on about how his life had changed once he had people to help him in the areas he needed to work on to improve himself in a variety of ways. This man had been through a lot during his life, as all of us have been, and yet he had emerged a happy and successful person. This man was Raymond Aaron, the person I consider to be my first mentor as I began my new life. I have already mentioned him in two earlier sections of this book.

On that morning of April, 2005, Raymond taught me that I had made the mistake of thinking that I could do everything alone by believing that I was an island. Once I made that mental shift to embracing the idea of allowing others to help me, my life began a transformation that continues to this day and will until I take my final breath.

His Monthly Mentor™ program is one I still use to this day. By setting annual, quarterly, and monthly goals, and breaking that down even further to my minimum, target, and 'outrageous' goals in each of several categories I am able to see measurable results of my daily actions. I would encourage you to find a goal setting and achieving program that works for you, and to write everything down on a daily and weekly basis to make sure you are headed in the right direction for what you would like to achieve. As the saying goes, there is nothing worse than watching someone running enthusiastically in the wrong direction.

Raymond and I continue to be friends, and he has even invited me to speak at several of his live events, including ones in Toronto, Canada and in London, England. Our relationship is a complicated one, where sometimes he is a big brother to me, while at other times he comes to me for advice and help with technology or marketing strategies that I have mastered by simplifying the process.

Think BIG every day, and do not share your ideas with others, even those close to you, until you have fleshed them out at least partially. This will help to keep them from being squashed under the thumbs of those who mean well but want to protect you from yourself. Wait until you can answer their questions, entertain their points of view, and defend your dreams and goals in a way that sounds like you have given them the time and thought they deserve.

Chapter 8
Making a Name for Yourself

What other people think of me
is none of my business.
~ Wayne Dyer

You may finally be seeing that much of what I'm sharing within the pages of this book is related to making a name for yourself. Setting yourself apart from others by laying a foundation on which you can build a solid business is something few people are willing to do. This is why following my three-pronged Trifecta approach with a book, a blog, and broadcasts is so powerful, and so worth the time and effort you will put into implementing it over time.

There are many people who have done this in a similar way to make their name a household word, at least in the circles where their topic is considered to be a valuable one. I know some of these people personally. I believe that by sharing their stories and using them as examples you can better decide which path is best for you.

I first met Bill Phillips when he was speaking at an event I attended back in 2005. He came across as arrogant at first, but once he began to share his story I resonated with his message. He had been a bodybuilder as a teenager growing up in Colorado. His father took him and his brother mountain climbing from an early age, and this gave him the inner strength and courage to go after goals others might think to be too big or too risky.

In his early twenties Bill decided to pursue weight lifting and bodybuilder as a vocation rather than simply a hobby, and for the next ten years he drifted from adventure to adventure, never having true meaning in his life and attracting many people who were not sincere and did not have his best interest at heart.

Finally he connected with people who gave him guidance as to what his future could be, and that led to him writing a book called *Body for Life*. This book went on to become a *New York Times* bestseller, and catapulted Bill to the top of his field as a thought leader in the area of fitness and nutrition. Everything changed as his life became one of service to others around the topic he had been involved in since he was a teen.

This took him to new heights as opportunities began to present themselves more easily than he ever thought possible. He moved to Los Angeles, where he became a sought after expert on films and television shows. When an actor or other person in the spotlight needed to get in shape quickly and healthfully, Bill's name was at the top of the list.

Most recently he has started hosting camps at his private gym in Golden, Colorado, and I have been a guest there on two separate occasions. This enables him to connect with people one on one and learn from them in a way he had lost touch with and continued to crave as he became better known over the years.

The point I am making with this story is that this is the perfect example of how you may change your life by focusing on your interests, gifts, and talents, getting the message of what you believe and have experienced out to the world, thereby making a name for yourself as an expert and credible authority on your topic. Anyone can achieve this goal, no matter where you are right now, how old you are, or what your previous life experiences have been.

Other examples of people who have used a similar strategy to build a solid business based on their topic are financial expert Suze Orman, virtual mentor Michael Hyatt, entrepreneur and angel investor Tim Ferriss, marketer Seth Godin, and relationship expert Dr. John Gray.

I continue to do this with my experience and expertise as an online marketing strategist. Once I understood the power of becoming an author, blogging consistently, and broadcasting my information through audios and videos, my life became easier and simpler as the people who wanted to connect with me were able to find me and learn from me in a way that would best serve their own needs and desires. Like magic, everything came together in a way I had only dreamed of and my business blew up (this is a good thing, if you aren't familiar with this saying!).

How Do I Want Others To Think Of Me?

I began this chapter with a quote from Wayne Dyer that states, 'What other people think of me is none of my business.' With that said, remember that you are the one that builds your reputation one day and one action at a time. So the only question to ask yourself now is 'What name do I want to make for myself?' I highly recommend that you take the time and make the effort to think this through and write down your thoughts about this aspect of what I am teaching and sharing with you over the next few days. Ask yourself these questions:
- ✓ What do I most want to be known for in my lifetime?
- ✓ Which area of my life am I most proud of when it comes to my experiences and accomplishments?
- ✓ How can I best serve others as they strive to reach their own goals and dreams?
- ✓ When I ask the people who know me best to tell me what my areas of strength are, what do they say?

✓ What is the legacy I wish to leave behind for future generations?

Being Controversial

Controversy is a very good thing. While I'm not saying to disagree with others just to be contrary, thinking of yourself as contrarian will definitely work in your favor over time. I'll give you an example of how this worked for me as I grew my online business.

Everyone who starts out as an entrepreneur starts with an empty database of prospects and clients. I met a few people early on, primarily at local events and in groups I was associated with, but my list grew at a snail's pace that first year. However, my income continued to grow as I learned more and had more products and services to offer for sale.

At some point I heard someone say that you needed at least ten thousand names on your list before you could make any real income. At that point I had just under a thousand people in my database and had already reached six figures a year. This was my comment when this marketer spouted off at a live event we were both attending about what he believed to be the undisputed truth:

"I'm sure glad I never got that memo, because I make very good money with my very small list."

If you remember what I said earlier, back in the section on Authorship in Chapter 2, this would become a part of my branding and became my first bestselling book.

As the saying goes, 'Love me, hate me, there's no money in the middle.' It has been my experience that this is true in many walks of life. Stand up for yourself and say what you think and believe and it will serve you well over time.

Now it's time to get down to the nuts and bolts of creating your entrepreneurial Trifecta. In the next section I'll explain in great detail how to write a full length book, how to set up and grow an authority blog, and how to use a variety of broadcasting platforms to build a business based upon your experience, interests, and area of knowledge and expertise.

Let's get started!

Section IV

How Do You Write a Book, Blog, and Broadcast?

Chapter 9
How to Write Your Book

*The most important people in the publishing process
are the writer and the reader. All others are
superfluous at this point in time
and looking forward.*
~ Connie Ragen Green

This is my twelfth published book. It still astonishes me to write that statement, as I was the person who wanted to write for decades and seldom followed through with any of my ideas.

I began this chapter with a bold statement I made back in 2012. It continues to be true and is why people like you and me can be so very successful with an online business. What I have learned over the past five or six years is the key to how you can do what I have done, and even go beyond my results.

It begins by acknowledging the three steps you absolutely must take in order to write a book, create a course or information product, or achieve most any goal that requires at least some type of writing. These steps are:

- ✓ Organize your thoughts in a clear and concise manner
- ✓ Prepare a detailed and complete outline
- ✓ Schedule the time you will write every day

Perhaps these steps appear to be an oversimplification of the process, but suffice it to say they have enabled me to grow a business that has helped me to change my life, become a sought after speaker and respected authority in the world of online marketing, and to build an online empire where I am able to serve other entrepreneurs all over the planet. Yes, it's that simple and that powerful. Let's go into more detail on each of the steps now.

Organizing Your Thoughts

Organizing your thoughts is the first part of this process, and one that I was used to doing over the years. I would spend endless hours daydreaming and planning out what I would write about or create. Many times I would do this while on a walk out in nature, at the beach, or even in the shower. You may have similar experiences you can relate to here.

What kept me from moving on to the next step and achieving my writing goals was one thing, and one thing only; I never took the time to write down my thoughts in an organized way. They say that the dullest pencil is better than the sharpest mind, which means that we must write down our ideas and continue to revisit, revise, and rewrite them over time if we are to accomplish anything worthwhile in our lives. Once I understood that and began to make notes that turned into fully fleshed out ideas I was on my way to success. This spilled over into other areas of my life as well, enabling me to complete projects I had long since abandoned.

Start with a notebook or a word processing document and begin documenting your thoughts and ideas for your book. I'll be teaching you a four question process later on that will make this even easier, but for now I want you to simply write down what your book will be about and any information you know for certain you would like to include in the final manuscript.

Creating an Outline

The second step in this process is to create your outline. I fought this for so many years, even though people I knew of and respected were recommending it based on their own experiences. Once I took all of my ideas for a book and turned them into outline format, my book was ready to almost write itself. Please don't think for a moment that I am exaggerating or overstating the value of having a tight outline. This strategy works!

Divide your outline into sections, and then divide each section into chapters. Further divide each chapter into sub-sections, and you will have the basis for an excellent book. I'll give you some concrete examples of this in just a moment.

For this book that you are now reading, I had presented much of the information while speaking at events earlier in the year, so my PowerPoint presentation became a part of what I incorporated into my outline as well.

Scheduling Time to Write Every Day

The third step is to schedule the time to write each day. Based on my experience, and that of the many students with whom I've had the opportunity to work closely with over these past several years, if you do not demand this part of the equation of yourself you will not succeed and you'll live with the frustration of not reaching your goals for eternity.

I've written quite a bit on the idea of 'prime time' in our lives and for our businesses. This originally came from network television, where prime time was Monday through Friday from seven until eleven in the evening. This was considered to be the peak broadcasting time, where most of the viewing audience was in front of their television sets and advertisers would have the best chance of having their commercials viewed by the most people. Once we began recording our favorite television programs and having so many alternative choices for entertainment, this all changed, but I digress.

You must figure out when your own 'prime time' occurs. It turns out that I am the most alert early in the mornings, so it makes sense that I would write and create products during those hours. While I was still working as a classroom teacher, I was at school during those morning hours five days a week, so I took advantage of Saturday and Sunday mornings to write my blog posts, articles, and emails to my list, as well as to create information products.

Because your productivity will be heightened during these peak hours, you will find that you accomplish quite a bit more in fewer hours this way. These days I guard my mornings and still make sure I have at least two hours to write four or five days each week.

Make this an appointment with yourself that you are not likely to break, and also let people close to you, especially those living with you, know that you are deep in thought and hard at working during your 'prime time' hours. Ask them to respect you by not disturbing you during this time. I have found that by being honest about what I need I'm able to get full cooperation from those close to me.

The Writing Process

The actual writing of your book should flow seamlessly after you have created a tight outline and know exactly what each Section, Chapter, and Sub-Section will be about. I have shared that my very first book, *Huge Profits With a Tiny List: 50 Ways to use Relationship Marketing to Increase Your Bottom Line* was written by repurposing fifty blog posts I published on my blog. This 'blog your book' method is not a new one; people were already doing this successfully several years before I published that first book. But it took me time to understand the fact that making an outline would make it all so much easier.

Each blog post became the focus for that topic I was addressing, and my goal was to write at least five hundred words about it, first for my blog and later for the book.

If you find yourself getting stuck at any point, go back to your outline and make sure that each of your chapters has three sub-sections that make sense. Then spend time each day writing as much as you can about the topic of that particular sub-section. Research as necessary to fill in any gaps in your knowledge and/or experience. The world is at our fingertips when it comes to accessing information on anything at all.

The Four Questions

I was first introduced to the four questions by my friend and colleague Alex Mandossian. He shared that he used these questions as the basis for much of what he was doing in his business and I wanted to explore the idea of doing the same thing.

Several years later I was deep in discussion with transformational coach Miguel de Jesus and he brought up something that reminded me of these questions. When we explored it further it turned out that there was a connection, as there often is when you spend time with like-minded people.

WHY is (YOUR TOPIC) so important for our audience to learn more about?

WHAT is (YOUR TOPIC) by definition?

WHAT IF our community utilized the strategies you are teaching us about (YOUR TOPIC), what would their life be like in 30 days, 90 days, 1 year?

HOW does (YOURTOPIC) work in a step-by-step process?

The Four Questions have been discussed by several people over the past several years, most notably Simon Sinek and David Kolb.

Simon Sinek has a theory that "People don't buy what you do; they buy why you do it. And what you do simply proves what you believe." His main work is found in *Start with Why: How Great Leaders Inspire Everyone to Take Action*.

David Kolb adheres to the philosophy "Tell me, and I will forget. Show me, and I may remember. Involve me, and I will understand." from Confucius. His main work is at *Experiential Learning: Experience as the Source of Learning and Development*.

Advanced Strategies for Creating Your Outline

Even though I address everything contained within this chapter in much greater detail in my previous book, *Write. Publish. Prosper. How to Write Prolifically, Publish Globally, and Prosper Eternally*, I do intend to give you what you need here in this book so that you can move forward more quickly and easily. Here is how to create an outline that will allow you to keep moving, to the point that it will finally seem as though your book is writing itself.

Big Idea - What is your premise for this topic?

Title - Your Working Title (This will most likely be changed at some point in your writing process.)

Foreword - Who should write this for you? I recommend that it be someone who has known you for some time and has seen your transformation from where you were to where you are now in your life and in relation to your topic. This is the place for your guest author to show the reader why they should be reading this book. The foreword of a book is a major selling tool for the book. If it is written properly, and by the appropriate person, the book's author will gain a lot of credibility in the reader's eyes. Remember that the author of the book should never write the foreword.

Preface - Your Story: Journey of Pain into Pleasure - Before, After, After. For example, I was a classroom teacher who also worked in real estate and dreamed of having more time and money to live a different kind of life. That's my 'before'. My 'after' is that I walked away from my previous life by resigning from the school district and giving away my best real estate clients and started an online business. This is good, but it's incomplete. My second 'after' is that I now earn about ten times as much income as before, while working only about twenty-five percent as much as I did before. The preface is a place for the book's author to tell the reader how this book came into being, and why. It should build credibility for the author and the book.

The Acknowledgements section is where you recognize and thank the people who have been helpful in your process of writing your book, either directly or indirectly. This could include your family, editor, illustrator, graphic designer, mentor, and publisher. Instead of simply acknowledging them, briefly explain the reason(s) why you have mentioned them.

Introduction - Your Thesis Statement

Sections (Based on the 4 Questions)

The titles of each chapter. Take the time to brainstorm your chapter title ideas, knowing that you may add others later on and eliminate those that don't work well for your topic. It's your book and you will make all of these decisions.

The premise, or Big Idea, of each chapter. Each chapter must be able to stand on its own and fit well into the scheme of things as you unfold your ideas and information.

Now you will reorganize your chapters to put them into the logical order of your book. I can now do this within my word processing document, but in the beginning I would write them down on strips of paper and lay it all out on my dining room table until it made sense for me.

Next, choose two or three to fit into each of your four or five sections.

If you need more ideas, go back to Amazon and do some additional research.

The final step for this part of the process is to go one level deeper with your outline.

For each chapter, write three sentences that can be starting points for your writing. We will refer to these as the Chapter Sub-Sections.

The Dedication is a special page where you thank the person or people who have made a difference to you. Here are some examples:

Simple – "This is for you, Mom."

Formal, with an anecdote – 'This book is dedicated to Mary Smyth, for her kindness and devotion, and for her endless support when Jane was ill; her selflessness will always be remembered.'

In Memory Of – 'In memory of John Smyth. You left fingerprints of grace on our lives. You shan't be forgotten.'

I dedicated my first book to my Mother, a close childhood friend who had recently passed away, and to my Rotary Club for their support as I changed my life. Remember there is no right or wrong way to do this, so write from your heart and you'll be ahead of the game.

Here is the proper order of things for your book:

Dedication

Table of Contents

Foreword

Preface

Acknowledgements

Introduction

Sections/Chapters

End Matter (as opposed to Front Matter)

The End Matter could consist of:

Epilogue

Afterword

Conclusion

Postscript

Backward (my own invention!)

Appendix(es)or Addendum

These are all optional, so you make the decision about what you will include.

You can now see that it is imperative to understand the basic differences in these book sections in order to produce a professional looking and complete book. Each section is clearly different from the others, and each performs a specific function in your book. Therefore, as an author you will need to put a lot of thought and effort into producing these vital sections.

The Power of Storytelling

I will end this chapter with a discussion of something that is so underutilized, yet so important in everything we do as entrepreneurs. It is storytelling.

We remember the people and places in our lives by the stories that are told about them. This even applies to historical figures, such as the story of Abraham Lincoln walking several miles to return someone's change they forgot to take while he was working at the general store as a young man.

These stories serve as a means by which we remember and share the qualities of the person they are about. Allow me to give you a personal example of this.

I attended a live event in the fall of 2008, when I had been online for less than two years. As we gathered in front of the conference room at the hotel in Los Angeles where this was happening (the same hotel I have now used to host two of my own events – this is another story!) a small circle of people next to me were talking about someone who had been a teacher and was now a successful entrepreneur. As I leaned in to hear more about this person, I finally realized they were talking about me. People who had not met me in person, and therefore did not recognize me were sharing stories with each other that I had originally shared through my blog posts, email messages, and teleseminars.

So, what's your story? Think about this over some time so that you can decide exactly what you wish to share about yourself with the world. Here are some questions to answer about yourself:

- ✓ How does my current lifestyle – job, family, experiences – relate to what I will be doing in my online business?
- ✓ How do my family members and close friends feel about my sharing their stories, as they relate to me?
- ✓ What are some of my beliefs and values that could be explained through stories?

Chapter 10
Setting Up Your Blog

Put your heart, mind, and soul into even your smallest acts.
This is the secret of success.
~ Swami Sivananda

As I discussed earlier, back in Chapter 2, blogging has been on the radar of the online world since just after the turn of the century. Now we have many options, in my opinion too many as to how we set up our blogs, and that's where all of the confusion arises. This is probably the area most people come to me for most often, and my advice has been the same for several years now and is not likely to change any time soon.

Earlier I stated that your blog is 'your home on the Internet' and that because of this fact you must own and control the real estate upon which it sits. What this means is that you must have your own hosting account where you can install, or have someone install for you a hosted WordPress site. Allow me to elaborate on this concept.

There are several free blogging platforms where you may quickly and easily set up your blog and then write posts to your heart's content. The difficulty arises when the owners of this virtual real estate decide that you have violated the terms of service and shut you down without warning. All of your hard work is destroyed and you are back at square one with your online business.

This is the example I share with my own students and mentees:

Just imagine that you are strolling through your local shopping mall and the leasing manager approaches you for a chat. He tells you that there is a kiosk that is currently unoccupied and that he had heard you were looking for a place to sell handbags. He offers you the use of this kiosk, situated in a highly trafficked area for as long as you need it, until someone else comes along that would like to lease it on a long term basis. This sounds like a wonderful opportunity to you and early the next morning you show up with your handbags and begin arranging them for all to see.

Business is booming and the holiday season is approaching. Shoppers love what you have to offer and tell their friends and neighbors. It's all you can do to keep your kiosk stocked and you feel like you have finally achieved great success with your business over these past several months.

The following Friday afternoon the leasing manager stops by for a chat. He waits until your customer has left and then informs you that someone has just signed a lease for the kiosk. Your kiosk. Your only place of business for the past several months. He asks if you can pack up your inventory, take down your signs, and clear out by nine o'clock that evening. Still in shock, you humbly nod 'yes' and begin taking your handbags and other belongings out to the car.

The following morning the new person is busily setting up their items when someone stops by to ask where the lady who was selling handbags at this location has moved to now. The new person has no idea and simply shrugs her shoulders. You stay home all weekend wondering what you will do now and where you went wrong with your business.

I hope this story adequately illustrates what I am talking about, as the scenario will be much the same if you do not own and control your blog. And the solution is a simple and inexpensive one, so there is no reason to do it any other way from the very beginning.

Start out by getting a hosting account. I have some recommendations at the end of this book in the *Resources* section. The next step is to purchase a domain where your new blog site will live. Long ago we used keywords for our blog's domain, but over these past several years it became more advantageous to use your name for this.

My name was not available when I first came online. Another woman named Connie Green was using it for her site on fashion design. I joked at that time that no one would ever confuse us because fashion has never been a priority of me. When I contacted her she offered to sell the domain ConnieGreen.com to me for a thousand dollars, but that was way out of my reach at that time. Instead, I began using my middle name, Ragen, and purchased ConnieRagenGreen.com to use for my new WordPress site. Simultaneously, I went over to my domain registrar and put in something called a 'back order' on the ConnieGreen.com domain. Within a year the other lady let the domain go and I was able to pick it up for under ten dollars.

This is yet another example of being proactive as an entrepreneur. If something is standing in your way, look for ways to work around the problem and accomplish your intended goal.

Your WordPress Dashboard

WordPress has evolved over the years to the point where it is now extremely user friendly. This platform is known as CMS, which stands for Content Management System. The definition of CMS is 'a computer application that allows publishing, editing and modifying content, organizing, deleting as well as maintenance from a central interface'.

From your hosting account you will install (or have someone else install) your WordPress site with just a few clicks. Your hosting company should be happy to walk you through this process.

You will then log in to what is known as your 'Dashboard', and that is where you have complete control over every aspect of your WordPress sites. I will cover just a few of the features and applications here.

WordPress started out as a free and open-source content management system based on PHP and MySQL. It was released in 2003 by its founders, Matt Mullenweg and Mike Little. I've included more information on this in the *RESOURCES* section at the end of this book.

I met Matt Mullenweg at the very first Blog World Expo conference in Las Vegas in the fall of 2007. At that time I was still using Typepad as my blogging platform because WordPress was just too technical for me. I spoke with Matt briefly and shared my thoughts with him, so I'd like to take credit for the changes that have been made to it over the years. However, it was most likely the collective thoughts of the bloggers on the now more than sixty million websites using WordPress that continue to be responsible for the changes.

In your Dashboard you will see that you have many choices, and I would encourage you to just click around and see what you discover. Remember that you can Google anything you have questions about and find the information you need. YouTube will usually have a video tutorial on most anything you need to learn as well. Start by going over to WordPress.org and clicking on the various menu items to learn more.

Plugins allow you to turn your WordPress site into a custom website at the click of your mouse. My colleague Adrienne Dupree and I created a course on the top 20 WordPress plugins for business in which we share our top picks. Most plugins are available for free installation, while some of the more sophisticated ones are paid. These are the three that I believe you absolutely cannot be without:

1) Yoast WordPress SEO – It allows you to optimize each page or post for a specific keyword phrase, making your blog more easily found by the search engines for the phrases that relate most closely to your site's topic. The author is Joost de Valk, a developer from the Netherlands who is highly respected online. The phonetic pronunciation of his first name, Joost, is Yoast, hence the name of his business.

2) Google Analyticator - Easily view your Google Analytics and real-time statistics inside WordPress. This makes it super simple to add your tracking code to find out everything about who is visiting your site, where they are coming from, and so much more.

3) Captcha - This plugin allows you to implement super security captcha form into web forms. WordPress continues to suffer attacks from hackers, and this plugin makes a huge difference.

Less is definitely more when it comes to plugins, so choose wisely and only add one plugin at a time to your blog to make sure there won't be any conflicts with your other plugins or your theme.

Themes in WordPress are the 'skin' of your site. This means that because of the Content Management System used in WordPress, your content will never be altered or deleted when you change over to another theme. There are both paid and free themes, so again I would direct you to the WordPress.org site to learn more about this.

Content Creation Strategy

The most important thing I can share with you about blogging, based on my now almost ten years of experience, is that consistency is the key. In the beginning it may feel as though you are lacking in knowledge on your topic, or just don't know what to say, but the process of 'finding your voice' will be a valuable one. Decide right now how often you will commit to writing and publishing a post and then stick to that schedule. Even if it feels as though you are slogging your way through a sea of molasses wearing heavy winter clothing, keep at it until writing on a regular basis becomes more comfortable and natural for you.

During the year I started my online business I was still teaching school, and intended to see the year through until the end of June. I needed time to write my blog posts and everything I tried seemed to fail. I was just too tired in the evenings, and I could only do so much on the weekends because of my real estate business. I had energy early in the mornings but needed to leave my house before six in order to beat the traffic down to my school.

I decided that getting to school a little early and writing at my desk would be an excellent idea, but on the very first day I had two people interrupt me before I could finish a paragraph. The next day I sat in my car in the parking lot to write, but several minutes later another teacher arrived and waited for me to get out of the car and walk into the building with her.

That's when I had a bright idea that ended up working out quite well for the remainder of the school year. I kept a box at the post office located about a mile from my school, and I would pull in to the parking lot, get out of the car and go in to pick up my mail. Then I would sit there for the next half hour writing in my notebook. I could create at least one blog post each morning, as well as make some notes on other things I was working on to build my business. On the following Saturday morning I would simple copy from my notebook into my blog and schedule the posts to go out over the next several days. Sometimes I would be in the classroom and would glance up at the clock and smile, knowing that my latest post had just gone live.

We build up a body of work with our writing one day, one idea, and on post at a time. Be willing to do the work and you will reap the rewards.

Chapter 11
Your Broadcast
Channels

"Remember Red, hope is a good thing, maybe
the best of things, and no good thing ever dies."
~ Andy Defresne to Ellis 'Red' Redding
in The Shawshank Redemption

If you have seen the film *The Shawshank Redemption*, and I highly recommend that you do take the time to see it, then you are familiar with the quote I have begun this chapter with and why it is decidedly apropos.

Broadcasting your message to the world is the way to reach people all over the planet quickly and easily. The fact that we can do this so inexpensively and sometimes even for free is still miraculous to me. Add to that the ease of the technology and you have a way to connect with people and market to them all as a part of your daily activities as an online entrepreneur.

I started with YouTube at least five years ago. I could use my hundred dollar Flip camera, now no longer in production, and upload videos within minutes using my laptop computer. About two years ago I began using my iPhone for all of my videos, and any smart phone is now just as simple.

Podcasting is another way to broadcast, and I first explored this in 2007. Believe it or not, I spoke for almost half an hour on the benefits of healthy eating, something I am definitely not an expert on. This recording was available on iTunes for several years before I deleted it and set up a podcast for my business at the end of 2011. I now have two successful podcasts, and one of them was named by Small Business Trends as one of the Top 100 Podcasts for Small Business in 2014.

There are now more ways than ever to broadcast and even live stream to the world. Recent additions to this are Periscope and Blab, and by the time you are reading this there will be even more opportunities to reach people who will be interested in you and what you are doing in regards to your niche topic.

The issue then becomes how to best utilize this type of technology to your greatest benefit so that your time is well spent and you get the results you are after.

Broadcasting to Build Your Business

You must first decide the format of what you will share with your audience. I believe this is crucial to your success and helps you to establish boundaries within your business. By this I mean that it is all too easy to fall into the habit of being available to your audience in a way that makes them feel like they are getting everything they need from you without having to spend any money with you. Why would they buy your books or your products when they can ask you anything they need to know on a regular basis?

Instead, choose a format that makes you accessible but not available. It's your business, so you must decide what works best for you.

For example, one of my podcasts is an interview series, where I invite guests to speak one on one with me for twenty to thirty minutes. I showcase them by allowing them to share exactly who they are and what they have to offer to the world. I've now hosted more than a hundred of these interviews, and the results have been nothing short of fantastic. Both my guests and I continue to build credibility and visibility, and many times I am invited to be a guest on other podcasts because of what I do on my own. The interview format is an excellent one.

My other podcast is one in which I answer questions and share information with my listeners. These are done as live teleseminars to begin with, and then posted at AskConnieAnything.com.

These calls give the people on my list the opportunity to get a shout out for their name and website while on the live call, and then for many years to come in my archived podcasts over at iTunes. This is a huge opportunity and I am always amazed at how few people take full advantage of it. You never know who might be listening at some point in the future and have an interest in exactly what you have to offer.

So these are examples of the interview style and questions and answer format for podcasting. You may also want to keep it light and use a format I like to refer to as 'edutainment'. This is where you educate your audience on your topic, while also keeping them amused and entertained. Perhaps I incorporate that into everything I do with storytelling, as our stories show that we are human and help people to understand us on a deeper level.

Setting up and maintaining a YouTube Channel will also massively increase your credibility and visibility, all while helping you to build your business. I describe mine as a 'lifestyle' Channel because I show what I'm doing in various places around the world as a result of having a successful online business.

It's so simple these days to record short videos and upload them to YouTube right from your smart phone. I prefer to do them outdoors in remote locations and then wait until I am plugged in and connected to the Internet to upload them. This allows for High Definition video that provides a better quality and user experience.

In addition to podcasting and videos, it is now possible to host a live stream from your smart phone on platforms such as Periscope and Blab. Experiment with these to see what works best for your niche topic. I have found that limiting them to ten minutes or so and discussing a specific topic draws the most responsive audience. Make sure to always say your name and your website at the beginning and end of these live streams so people will be more likely to remember who you are and visit your site to get more information. And know that this ability to broadcast via live stream is amazing technology that was not available in this way even a year ago without having to set up expensive equipment and have technical assistance every step of the way. I love how the Internet continues to progress!

Interviews and Interviewing

Finding the right people to interview for your podcasts and other platforms, as well as finding others who will interview you must become a part of your ongoing business strategy.

To get booked as a guest for radio interviews, you'll want to find programs that regularly feature topics like those that you hope to promote on the air. Use Google or more specialized industry directories to find radio programs, podcasts, and even TV programs that book guests with knowledge and expertise like yours.

You'll want to reach the proper person, and this person is usually called a producer or a booker. For smaller podcasts and radio shows, this may actually be the same person. But for the larger ones, especially those that are nationally syndicated, guest experts are rarely contacted and then booked for interviews by the host. Read the show website, go through radio industry trade sites and magazines, and also listen to the radio show itself to learn who is the best person to approach for a guest interview appearance.

Remember that everything is about relationships, so start building those with people you may want to connect with in the future. Keep in mind that these people are most likely receiving dozens of interview pitches each day, so it's your job to be helpful and position yourself and your expertise as a potential solution problem of finding the right people for guest expert interviews. Try first to contact them via email, voice phone, or even by fax. Social media has helped me to reach many people, so go to Facebook, Twitter, and LinkedIn to find the people you need.

You must demonstrate your expertise first, so offer to be a guest expert whenever you see the radio show covering topics where you would fit well. Also, demonstrating your awareness of current events and the kinds of stories that show typically covers can help you position yourself as a helpful problem solver. These shows don't want to interview you just to promote your products, book, or live events. They are in the news business and want great content to share with their listeners. You will get more interviews if you tie your pitch to topics that are currently trending in the news, rather than focusing exclusively on trying to sell your product using their air time.

Here is a 'booking sheet' template you may wish to use when you are going after guest interviews:

Date
Time (and time zone)
Live or taped?
Name of show
Show website
Name of host
Name of producer
Contact details
Number to call, or will they call you?
Backup number
Duration of interview

If live, will they take questions from listeners?
If recorded, when and where will show air?
Will it be archived so you may link/download it later?
Any other relevant information

Use this as a guide and make any modifications you deem necessary as this part of your business begins to grow.
Social Media for Entrepreneurs

This seems like a good time to discuss the role of social media in your business. Entrepreneurs are fortunate to have the various platforms in which to share their message with the world in this way. This is a relatively new phenomenon.

The 'Big Three' of social media continue to be Facebook, Twitter, and LinkedIn. However, Pinterest, Google Plus, and Instagram have now forged a place in my heart and in my bottom line. Make sure you have set up each of these and completed your profiles as well.

My motto in regards to social media continues to be 'get in, get out, and get back to work!' Even after all of these years, I still find myself easily sucked into threads of Facebook and checking out status updates on the other sites. Automating as much of your social content as possible continues to be the best strategy, although manually posting your updates will most definitely bring you more engagement. I prefer a combination of both, thereby giving me both the satisfaction of knowing that I'll have a presence no matter what and the opportunity to connect on a more personal level with my followers and friends.

Also, think of social media as a venue to grow your business instead of as one where you will visit with family and friends. I made that distinction from the very beginning and it has paid off handsomely. If someone can call me on my home phone, visit my house, or is related to me, I truly do not need to be connected with them on the social media sites.

When I think back to my first few years working online it now seems like the Dark Ages. Facebook was still used primarily by college students, Twitter was not yet created, and LinkedIn was aimed at the corporate world. By 2008 this had all changed and online entrepreneurs were able to jump into the waters of visibility and credibility from behind their computers. Now that we have additional sites, such as Google Plus, Instagram, and Pinterest it seems like the world is our oyster when it comes to sharing content of all types with our prospects and clients.

Leverage the power of social media by making sure you are the one calling the shots. What I mean by this is that you only want to do what is comfortable for you. I prefer email to being messaged on Facebook, for example, and I let people know that right away. Also, my goal is to be the one starting most of the threads I comment on so that I am seen as the thought leader on the topic. This isn't a power struggle, but rather a way for you to assert yourself and to share your expertise in a way that can build up your business significantly over time.

Your Broadcasting Plan of Action

You must have a strategy for growing your business with broadcasting, so I recommend making a schedule and sticking to it. Start by fleshing out your profiles on each of the sites I have discussed here, and then use a printed or digital calendar to keep track of what you want to achieve.

Because there are now so many sites, I look for ways to repurpose everything I write, say, or film. This means that I will host a short Periscope episode and then post that on Facebook and Twitter, as well as uploading it to YouTube. When I post to either of my blogs I post that to LinkedIn and Twitter simultaneously, as well as to Facebook both manually and automatically.

As far as creating a broadcasting schedule, start out by writing down what you will do over the next two weeks. For me, that would include hosting one podcast, creating two short videos for YouTube, and hosting two Periscopes or Blabs.

Then write down what you will be talking about on each of these. Instead of talking about your overall general topic, niche it down a bit and choose just a small piece of your knowledge and expertise to share with others. For example, I might talk about the importance of creating and repurposing content, or how affiliate marketing fits into my overall business plan, or any of a number of other topics. The idea here is to give people something to think about and to remember you for as you share your experiences with them.

Embrace the idea of letting the world know who you are and what you have to say on your topic, and it will soon become a more comfortable way for you to connect with your prospects and to share your knowledge and expertise.

Section V

What's Next?

Chapter 12
Teaching Your Topic

*There is no scarcity of opportunity to make a living
at what you love; there's only scarcity of
resolve to make it happen.*
~ Albert Einstein

As a former classroom teacher of twenty years turned online entrepreneur, I view the act of teaching in a unique way and with a perspective that hopefully will make you think and act differently as you build your business. Time will tell whether this is true for you or not.

During my teaching career it was not unusual for me to have students with diverse backgrounds and experiences sitting side by side in my classroom. Academically, I could have someone who was labeled EMR (Educable Mentally Retarded) in the same class as someone involved in the GATE (Gifted And Talented Education) program. This was in my elementary school classes, where I primarily taught children in the fifth or sixth grades, making them eleven or twelve years old at the beginning of the school year.

It was my goal to make sure that each child in my class receives a quality education during the year they were with me, and not simply to become a year older. To that end, I had to be creative with my teaching strategies so that everyone would be served at the level where they were at that time. I did not have a Special Education credential, nor did I want to teach special needs students exclusively. Instead, I was a general education teacher, with supplemental credentials in science and mathematics, who simple wanted to offer every student who came through my classroom door the opportunity for a world class education.

Learning Modalities

This is when I learned more about the different learning modalities and how they affected the learning process. Modalities refer to how students use their senses in the learning process. We commonly consider there to be four primary modalities, including: visual (seeing), auditory (hearing), kinesthetic (moving), and tactile (touching). As you might surmise, the more senses or modalities we can activate, the more learning will take place.

The overwhelming majority of students are able to learn using all four of the modalities, but we all have preferences that can be capitalized on, as well as weaker leanings that can be enhanced. Traditional classrooms rely heavily on auditory stimulation with lecture and discussions taking priority, even though it is best to make every effort to attempt to create a learning environment that is conducive to all four modalities.

With almost forty students in my class, hosting a three-ring circus was not going to work for any of us. That's when I began to utilize 'peer teaching' as a method of helping everyone learn while also incorporating socialization, leadership, and self-esteem into my teaching practice.

The way it worked was that I began with a focused activity, a directed lesson, modeling of what was expected, and guided practice, as was common using something called a '7 Step Lesson Plan'.

Typically, the same four or five students would get it right away, and others would catch up over the next fifteen to twenty minutes or so. Then there were the students who could not understand enough of what I was teaching to follow along well at all.

So what I would do was to pair up everyone in the class in a way that worked for their preferred learning modality and their academic level. My system became the model for what we did regularly at my grade level at that school, and the results were impressive. Almost everyone had a grasp of the subject matter in a way that moved them forward with their studies.

Your Topic as a Signature Course

These same principles were the foundation for teaching my first online course more than five years ago. I knew that a few of those who signed up would understand what I was teaching very quickly. Others would need more time, but would ultimately catch up at some point. And then there would be a few who did not understand what I was teaching, and would be hesitant to ask for help.

The idea is to create a course you will come to be known for, and make it the best possible experience for everyone involved. I started by teaching affiliate marketing, paired my students into something I call 'Project-Based Learning' partners, and then offered small group and one-on-one mentoring to those who wanted to learn at a higher level.

The concept behind project-based learning is not an original one from me. Instead, it was developed for use in education, specifically for the Kindergarten through twelfth grade population. PBL is a dynamic approach to teaching in which students explore real-world problems and challenges. With this type of active and engaged learning, students are inspired to obtain a deeper knowledge of the subjects they're studying. A project is meaningful if it fulfills each of two criteria. First, the students must perceive the work as personally meaningful, as a task that matters and that they want to do well. Second, a meaningful project fulfills an educational purpose. Well-designed and well-implemented project-based learning is meaningful in both ways. Here are the essential components:

- ✓ Key Knowledge, Understanding, and Success Skills - The project is focused on student learning goals, including standards-based content and skills such as critical thinking/problem solving, collaboration, and self-management.
- ✓ Challenging Problem or Question - The project is framed by a meaningful problem to solve or a question to answer, at the appropriate level of challenge.
- ✓ Sustained Inquiry - Students engage in a rigorous, extended process of asking questions, finding resources, and applying information.
- ✓ Authenticity - The project features real-world context, tasks and tools, quality standards, or impact – or speaks to students' personal concerns, interests, and issues in their lives.
- ✓ Student Voice & Choice - Students make some decisions about the project, including how they work and what they create.
- ✓ Reflection - Students and teachers reflect on learning, the effectiveness of their inquiry and project activities, the quality of student work, obstacles and how to overcome them.
- ✓ Critique & Revision - Students give, receive, and use feedback to improve their process and products.
- ✓ Public Product - Students make their project work public by explaining, displaying and/or presenting it to people beyond the classroom.

Teaching online in this way got me started with my own Mentor program for new online entrepreneurs who wanted and needed ongoing training and guidance. This was the beginning of a program I maintained for several years, where ninety percent of the members joined at the one hundred dollars a month level for group webinars only, and others joined years later at five thousand dollars a year and beyond for one-on-one coaching and additional help with product creation and promotion. Where they entered the program was dependent upon on their circumstances, their dedication, and their desire to become successful as entrepreneurs. My results were impressive, with more than eighty percent retention, and students who continued to work with me went on to become affiliates for my products, joint venture partners, and good friends.

Start from where you are and create an online course that can be delivered by teleseminar or webinar over a period of three to six weeks. Create an outline (I use these for everything I do, not only for the books I write) and then break it up into sections.

You will want to create a study guide participants can download and print out. I still have these types of handouts from courses I took almost ten years ago now. I keep them in a file folder box and continue to refer to them when I need the information that was taught.

The Offline Connection

Now I will share something with you that is worth more than everything else in this book combined, but only if you actually implement it. I believe that by adding a physical component to what you teach online you will not only enhance the learning experience for your students but will also set yourself apart from everyone else doing something similar in your marketplace. I refer to this as the 'offline connection'. Allow me to explain this idea further.

Long, long ago, before the Internet was even a gleam in anyone's eye there were courses offered through magazines, such as the *Reader's Digest*, *Good Housekeeping*, and *Woman's*

Day. You could learn how to draw, to write children's books, and even how to become a pilot (the written part of that, anyway), and how to play the guitar. These were all correspondence courses, meaning that you mailed in your application and a check for the entire course or for the first month and then the lessons would be delivered to your home every month. I actually knew someone who was taking the course on how to draw, and it was my experience with her that made me think of this more than twenty-five years later.

One day I was visiting when her next lesson arrived. It was during the summer and all three of her daughters were at home when the mail carrier brought it to the draw. It was wrapped in a plain brown box and when my friend opened it there was a brightly colored notebook, as well as a package of written materials wrapped in cellophane.

We all sat down at the kitchen table as she carefully unwrapped everything and laid it out in front of her. Then she instructed her oldest daughter to bring her 'art box' to her. This box contained all of the earlier lessons, and she went through it for a moment before pulling out another brightly colored notebook, two folders, a pad of drawing paper, and some colored pencils.

Over the next half hour or so we watched as she read part of the lesson, began drawing her picture (it was a cat sleeping on an outdoor swing) and held it up from time to time for us to see and to make our comments.

This was a fascinating process to me, as I had seen those same advertisements in *Reader's Digest* and several other magazine for years, yet I had never known anyone personally who was participating in one of them.

Then the true magic happened; my friend's husband came home from work and the youngest daughter ran up to greet him. He picked her up and as he was swinging her around she exclaimed, "Mommy's art lesson came today!"

He put his young daughter down and smiled from ear to ear. He wanted to see what his wife had drawn and to talk about it.

This part of the story is important. The husband was excited to see what his wife was working on because that made it real in his eyes. He was the family's breadwinner, and knowing what the monthly check was paying for made a difference to him. There was concrete proof that she was indeed enrolled in an art class with real lessons and real results.

Imagine doing this for your topic. Instead of delivering everything online via teleseminars, webinars, electronic written materials, audios, and videos, you could make a portion of your training available in physical form. Yes, it can be expensive to print and mail this type of content, but wouldn't it be worth it if the perceived value is so much greater? And the idea that the rest of the family can also be so involved is most definitely an added advantage.

Chapter 13
Going Mainstream

*There's one quality which one must possess to win, and
that is definiteness of purpose, the knowledge of what
one wants, and a burning desire to possess it.*
~ Napoleon Hill

The world of online marketing is actually quite a small one; knowing that you can reach an even greater audience must be your goal. We refer to this as 'going mainstream', and it means that we will work to get our name in front of people all over the planet from a variety of walks of life. It's easier than you may think to actually make this happen, but you must give it lots of thought and then map out a strategy to implement on a regular basis.

I was first able to do this for my own business when I started including community leaders as guests on my podcast series. These were typically people I met through my Rotary Club, and ones with whom I had begun to form a relationship. These people were so impressive to me because of their many years of service and dedication to the community and to the world. When I began interviewing them I learned even more about business and success and my listeners loved hearing from people they might otherwise not have ever known about.

What I did not anticipate was that this would make me more well known in my own community. I was living full time in Santa Clarita, California, as I did not start living part-time there and part-time in Santa Barbara, California until 2011. So at that time I was working from my home computer and getting more involved in several different charitable organizations in and around Santa Clarita.

It didn't take long for me to become something of a local 'celebrity'. Business owners and others were fascinated at my endeavors with entrepreneurship and I was excited to start sharing my story. I was asked to be a guest on several radio programs, interviewed by the local papers, asked to write a column for a local magazine (I still write for this one every single month), invited to speak at live local events, and even honored by the Arts Commission for my contributions to the community.

Soon I was attracting the attention of community leaders and finally I understood that I could expand my world by simply thinking more 'mainstream' instead of so 'niche market'. Then I spent time with my mastermind group to explore the ways I could best leverage this concept.

During our mastermind sessions I came to the conclusion that I needed to get back to my roots in order to best be perceived as an expert and an authority in the world of online marketing. None of us falls out of the sky and on to the Internet or into cyberspace. My background was in education and in real estate and I was ready to acknowledge that fact and use it to my advantage.

My first stop was at my local real estate board to see what I could find out. I continue to be a licensed real estate broker in the state of California and a member of the board because I am able do one or two transactions a year for close friends and family members and also to keep my group insurance plan through them.

When I got to the information desk I explained what I was doing and asked if I could present something on blogging and social media at an upcoming 'Lunch and Learn' event.

Even though the reception they gave me was lukewarm, they agreed to consider me as a trainer.

I should explain why the real estate board did not welcome this offer with open arms. Back in 2007 almost no one was blogging for their business, and it was definitely not encouraged for real estate professionals. In order to be seen as cutting edge, I was willing to be controversial in this arena.

When I was finally asked to speak some months later, the audience was smaller than anticipated and not that excited to hear what I had to say. But they listened politely to what I was sharing and even asked a few pertinent questions. I always look on the bright side, and this was also great experience for me to be presenting in front of a group. The two people who did find value in my presentation on blogging for realtors ended up signing up to be a part of a course that I was teaching at that time on the topic.

Be willing to check out anything that seems like a fit for your background and experience, even if it seems to go slowly at first. If you seek out opportunities to speak to groups that you are connected with through your offline life, this will be excellent for you as well.

Next I sought out ways to use my teaching experience as a way to build my business. The school districts were interested in learning more about technology at that time, but that was not my strong area of expertise. Instead, I chose to present information to teachers who were looking for ways to supplement their income and have something to do during their vacations and breaks from the classroom. In retrospect, I would have been better off presenting to them on the topics of productivity and time management, because I had obviously been strong in both areas while I was simultaneously working as a classroom teacher and staying active in real estate as a broker and an appraiser. But hindsight is always twenty twenty, and I did the best I could with what I knew and believed at that time.

A few years later, after I had published my very first book, my friend and mentor Raymond Aaron contacted me about speaking at his upcoming event. He was working with people who were new or aspiring authors, and I was introduced as an Internet marketer who could be trusted to guide them in the proper direction as they marketed their book to the world. That introduction definitely made me stand out in the crowd and allowed me to connect with people in a new and different way. That's when I truly understand the power of leveraging your knowledge within a much larger, hence 'mainstream' group.

I hope that you are understanding the value of what I am sharing with you here. Look back into your recent and more distant past and make a list of every group you have ever been a part of. It does not matter if you are currently a part of it, or if it has been many years since you were in contact with them. Do not forget to include religious groups, charitable foundations, and groups you were connected with because of someone else in your family (such as a musical group you helped out when your family member was in the high school band). Anything is possible when you keep an open mind and take appropriate action on a regular basis.

Publicity

The fastest way to go mainstream is to shout from the rooftops about what you are doing in your business. This is where publicity comes into the mix. I call it the 'Kindergarten Effect'.

If you have ever spent time with a new Kindergartner then you will relate to what I am saying here. They are surprised and amazed on an hourly basis at the new world that is unfolding around them. I taught this grade level two different years over my twenty year teaching career and can tell you that this was something that both thrilled and frustrated me throughout each of those years.

Children of this age will tell you stories of how a fly flew in through the classroom window and landed on someone's arm. The story continues as the fly then swooshes across the room, causing children to run for cover and squeal in both terror and delight until final exiting through another open window on the other side of the room. This event was a big deal and they want to share it with anyone who will listen.

Do the same thing for your business. Perhaps you believe that setting up a new blog or website is no big deal, but many others would disagree. We tend to take for granted the events in our life that seem mundane and routine, while others would see them as brilliant and monumental.

I did not fully appreciate this concept until I wrote and published my first book in 2010. My family, friends, and community members were beside themselves when they found out they were rubbing elbows with a published author. That's when I sprang into action with getting my publicity campaigns off the ground and into my business model.

Sending press releases is an excellent way to begin. Start by using one of the free press release services until you get into the flow of writing in this way, and then switch over to a paid service. I continue to use Web Wire for this, as their costs are more than fair for what they deliver.

Once your book is published, visit local bookstores to inquire about having a book signing. Each one will have a different policy, so make a list of all of the ones within driving range of your home and get busy talking with them. I like to bring about a half dozen books with me to leave with them, and because your book will have a bar code they will be able to sell them and keep the profit for themselves. This will cost you approximately twenty dollars and is worth every penny.

Your press releases should announce everything you do for your business, including starting a new site, creating a course or information product, or when you will be speaking to a group or at an event. Use my example of the

'Kindergarten Effect' to make every little action you take into a big deal that is newsworthy.

Writing for local, offline publications has also allowed me in get in front of a mainstream audience. I write columns for two publications and enjoy sharing my knowledge and expertise with the readers. The feedback I have received continues to be positive and the editors of these publications are happy to receive content for me that will enrich the experience of their audience.

Take some time now to think about how you can go mainstream with your online business.

Chapter 14
Your Marketing Strategy

Only you can control your future.
~ Dr. Seuss

Even though there is an inherent marketing aspect in the three-pronged approach outlined in this book, you must resign yourself to the fact that it is up to you to make things happen in your online business. Embracing marketing as a part of your daily activities will help you to enjoy the process of growing your business. Your actions play a pivotal role in your journey to success as an entrepreneur.

Most of us were raised to believe that it is not polite to brag about ourselves or to boast of our accomplishments. My mother had a saying, most likely rooted in her Midwest upbringing that went like this:

"The cream always rises to the top."

I guess this means that people will find out when you do a good job or are involved with something noteworthy, but that has not been my experience. Here is an example of that:

I was hosting a teleseminar years ago when I mentioned something about a blog post I had written. Someone on the call said, 'You have a blog?' I was shocked at his remark until I realized that he would have no way of knowing this unless I had mentioned it, not once but repeatedly over time.

That's when I decided to shout from the rooftops, both virtual and offline whenever I did even the smallest thing for my business.

Getting back to blog posts, here is what I do each time that I publish a new post:

- ✓ I go over to a site called Just Retweet and schedule my post to go out about a dozen times. This service works on a credit basis, but you may also purchase credits.
- ✓ Then I go over to Facebook and manually post the permalink to my post and something about it. Even though I use automated services, such as a third party application called Networked Blogs for this, it has been shown that you get much better user engagement when you post it yourself on your wall or page.
- ✓ The next stop is on LinkedIn, where I do a status update to share my post. I have my Twitter account connected there, so it will also post to Twitter on my behalf, saving me some time.
- ✓ Finally, I send out an email broadcast to my list, announcing the topic of my recent post and asking them to visit my blog, read my post, and to leave a comment.

The combination of all of these things leads to increased traffic, visitors, and interaction for each of my posts. All of this takes less than ten minutes after my post is written. If you get into the habit of doing this it will seem like second nature after a very short time.

When I record a podcast, I then turn that into a blog post and promote it in much the same way. Because of how the technology works with a plugin on my WordPress sites, visitors to my blogs may actually listen to them right on my site, even though I encourage everyone to go over to iTunes and to subscribe to my podcasts. I always mention my blog and my books on my podcasts so that listeners are aware of what I am doing.

My books are all available on Amazon, and I have included more information on this in the Resources section at the end of this book.

You can see that it is the connection between your blog(s), you podcast(s), and your book(s) that makes this strategy so powerful. Mention all that you do on each of these and it will increase your reach exponentially over time.

Building a Responsive List

This is the perfect time to have a more detailed discussion about the importance and steps required to build a list of prospects to grow your business. And even though I have built a reputation for making 'huge profits with a tiny list' the truth is that you will always want to market your business in such a way as to consistently grow your list and your income.

It's so true that the gold is in the list. The size of your list will dictate the leverage you will have in everything you do. So, how do you grow a highly responsive list, one that will open and read your emails, take your recommendations, and think of you as a thought leader in your niche?

By carefully building, maintaining, and nurturing your relationship with the people who come to you as their trusted advisor. This won't happen overnight, but over time you will find that these are the people who encourage you to move forward. Allow me to explain.

From the very beginning I have asked the people on my list to hit 'reply' to ask me their questions. It is from these email interactions that I have been able to connect with people more closely over the years. Some of the people have never met me in person at my own or someone else's live event, yet they join me for my open teleseminars and my online courses. Our virtual relationship has grown over time to the point where we know, like, and trust each other very much.

It all starts with your free giveaway, also referred to as an 'ethical bribe'. This is what you offer the visitors to your blog in exchange for their name and email address. I have seen this done in hundreds of variations, but I strongly believe that if you offer them a short report (somewhere between seven and fifteen pages, or about two thousand to five thousand words) in PDF (portable document format) and only ask for their first name and primary email address you will have the best results and the highest percentage of optins on a regular basis. You will want to experiment with this for your own niche, but this is an excellent starting off point. Do not ask them for their last name, phone number, or any other information until they have signed up and know you a little better.

The next thing is your autoresponder sequence, which consists of the emails you have already written and have set to go out once someone has joined your list. I recommend one a day for the first tem days, as this is when we are all the most excited about learning something new that we believe will be helpful to us in some way.

After the initial ten days of email messages, in which you share more information on your topic, allow them to hear your voice on a teleseminar or your podcast, invite them to read your blog posts, recommend your own and affiliate products, and ask them to hit 'reply' to ask you any questions they may have, I would then switch to two or three times a week for emails.

At this point you will begin sending your list regular broadcast messages. This was confusing for me in the beginning, so I attempt to give you a complete explanation of this now.

The difference between an autoresponder message and a broadcast message is that the former goes out automatically and the latter is sent in real time. For example, if I want to let people know about a new product that is being offered at a discount price, or a live call or event I am hosting, I must send out a broadcast email. On the other hand, if I want to tell them about my podcast series or a product that is always available at the same price, this can be included in an autoresponder email. So the autoresponders must contain content that is evergreen, whereas the broadcasts may or may not contain information that is time sensitive. I hope this clears up the confusion about the difference between these types of email messages.

Also, when someone opts in to your list they are on Day 1 of that sequence. If they are on Day 50 and you add an autoresponder message to your sequence and place it at Day 49, that person will not see it because they are past that point in the sequence. Do not worry about this, as your goal is to get more and more people to opt in and to then broadcast to those who have been with you for awhile.

If you send out a broadcast email message that generates a good response, meaning that you make lots of sales of whatever you are promoting or lots of traffic to the blog post you are sharing, then you may want to copy and paste that message into your autoresponder sequence. And remember that 'lots of' will mean something different to everyone.

Email marketing has its ups and downs, and no one seems to agree as to which autoresponder services work best, but suffice it to say that we will all continue to deliver our information in this way for some years to come. Make sure that your 'from' name is the name people will recognize when they first see your message in their inbox, as this is the number one determiner of whether they will click to open and read your message. The subject line is next in importance, and then the first sentence of your message that can be seen before they even open it.

The final comment I will make, for now anyway, on the important topic of list building is to remember why someone joined your list in the first place. I always say that most of the people on my list probably love animals and need to take off at least a few pounds. That doesn't mean they want to hear about dog training or weight loss from me.

Now let's talk about other ways to connect with your prospects, and even your current clients and customers. These methods and techniques and all time tested and proven to be effective, no matter which niche you are working in.

Setting Up an E-Course

I'm not the only one who loves e-courses. This refers to short courses that can be delivered electronically, hence the term e-course. Think of a series of lessons, broken up into several parts, and delivered over a five or seven day period. These lessons can all be set up in your autoresponder system to go out automatically once someone has opted in to that list.

Choose just one aspect of your topic so that each lesson can be just a few paragraphs in length and still teach the reader something significant on your topic.

Make sure to include clickable links in each of the lessons, letting them know that something is for sale. This can be books or other items on Amazon, your own products and courses, and affiliate offerings.

On about the third of fourth day, begin including a link for them to be able to download the entire e-course as a PDF. Even though they will continue to receive their daily lessons, they will no longer fear the possibility of not receiving all of them. We all crave completion in our lives.

At the end of the e-course, include a call to action as to what action you would like for them to take next, now that the course has been completed.

Relationship Marketing with Social Media

Social media marketing is more of relationship marketing, in my opinion, and I seldom offer anything directly for sale there. Instead, as I discussed earlier in this book, use your social media connections as a way in which you can more easily form relationships with your friends and followers than you could in person. Join groups, make comments, ask questions, and show people a more personal side of you for best results.

This does not mean that you have to share everything you are doing, or pictures of family members, but it does provide you the opportunity to let people know what you care about when you aren't involved in your business. For me, being able to share some of the projects I work on with the non-profits and other service organizations brings joy to my heart.

Chapter 15
What's Next For You?

We choose to go to the Moon in this decade and do
the other things, not because they are easy,
but because they are hard.
~ John F. Kennedy

If you are familiar with the quote I've included at the beginning of this chapter then you know the power it had on the people in the United States and ultimately throughout the world when President Kennedy gave that speech on September 12, 1962, as he spoke to a crowd of more than thirty-five thousand people at Rice Stadium in Houston, Texas. His goal was to persuade the American people to support the national effort to land a man on the Moon and return him safely to the Earth.

Here is an excerpt from the main part of that speech, penned by Ted Sorenson:

We set sail on this new sea because there is new knowledge to be gained, and new rights to be won, and they must be won and used for the progress of all people. For space science, like nuclear science and all technology, has no conscience of its own. Whether it will become a force for good or ill depends on man, and only if the United States occupies a position of pre-eminence can we help decide whether this new ocean will be a sea of peace or a new terrifying theater of war. I do not say that we should or will go unprotected against the hostile misuse of space any more than we go unprotected against the hostile use of land or sea, but I do say that space can be explored and mastered without feeding the fires of war, without repeating the mistakes that man has made in extending his writ around this globe of ours.

There is no strife, no prejudice, and no national conflict in outer space as yet. Its hazards are hostile to us all. Its conquest deserves the best of all mankind, and its opportunity for peaceful cooperation may never come again. But why, some say, the Moon? Why choose this as our goal? And they may well ask, why climb the highest mountain? Why, 35 years ago, fly the Atlantic?

We choose to go to the Moon! We choose to go to the Moon in this decade and do the other things, not because they are easy, but because they are hard; because that goal will serve to organize and measure the best of our energies and skills, because that challenge is one that we are willing to accept, one we are unwilling to postpone, and one we intend to win.

This speech uses three strategies that were crucial to reaching the goal:
1. a characterization of space as a beckoning frontier,
2. an articulation of time that locates the endeavor within a historical moment of urgency and plausibility,
3. and a final, cumulative strategy that invites audience members to live up to their pioneering heritage by going to the moon.

Why am I pointing all of this out within the context of a book on becoming a successful online entrepreneur? Because I wholeheartedly believe that we must adopt similar strategies if we are to succeed. We must decide what we want, strategize on how we can best achieve our goals, and then take action by implementing everything we are learning on a daily basis to make sure we arrive in a timely manner.

President Kennedy wanted the United States to land a man on the Moon, knew that many people would be needed in order to do this and that a huge amount of money would be needed, and wanted to spend the remainder of his life making this happen. He successfully made the case to taxpayers that NASA needed a $5.4 billion budget, an amount unheard of for any project up until this time. He also wanted all of the country's citizens to join him with their support, and that started on that day with the people who were there in the football stadium to hear him speak live. And on July 20, 1969 the goal was reached when Apollo 11 delivered astronauts Buzz Aldrin and Neil Armstrong to the surface of the Moon (a third astronaut aboard that spacecraft, Michael Collins, did not walk on the Moon's surface) and carried them safely back to Earth.

I'm not suggesting that what we do as entrepreneurs is akin to putting a man on the Moon, but aren't our hopes and dreams just as important in our minds? Then we must have a viable strategy and the hope and belief in our success.

I had all but given up on the hope of having a different life while I was teaching and working in real estate during my forties. I had settled for a life filled with mediocrity and chaos, a life where living month to month and paycheck to paycheck was my accepted existence. It wasn't until I met the couple I talk about earlier in Chapter 7 that I had a glimmer of hope in my thoughts and subsequent actions that led to everything that has followed and occurred during these past ten years of my life.

You must take back your life, reinvigorate your imagination, and know that anything is possible to fully understand what it's like to have hope in your heart and soul. For me, just the thought of starting a new business and being able to let go of my past life as a teacher and real estate broker was enough to open my mind to the possibilities. Following through with it and earning income from my home computer solidified the feeling and made it even stronger.

As I look back over the past ten years I realize that it was all about getting out of my comfort zone. My confidence and self-esteem were at an all time low when I left my teaching job, and it took time for me to have the courage to put myself out there as an online entrepreneur. Once I was willing to take some risks everything began to fall into place and I felt like a new person.

During the summer of 2006 I began attending Rotary meetings in the city I had recently moved to, Santa Clarita. Within a few months I saw the value of being a part of an international service organization and decided to become a member. It was at these meetings that I found the courage to begin speaking in front of groups, something I had feared all of my life. They say that the fear of public speaking is right up there with the fear of death, and I can certainly attest to that.

Over the next few months they thrust the microphone into my hand on many occasions and I was forced to talk to the group. At some point it became comfortable and even fun to have control over the group in that way and soon I was speaking to larger groups.

In 2008 I was asked to speak at an Internet marketing event and that's when I officially added public speaking to my list of accomplishments. Even though my speaking and selling from the stage was not very effective in the beginning, I was confident that it would improve over time. I now speak regularly at my own and other marketing events, at conferences and workshops for authors, small business owners, and entrepreneurs, at Rotary clubs, and even at churches and other civic organizations. I have spoken on three continents and love sharing my message and expertise in this way.

I would encourage you to do this as well. In the beginning I was told that public speaking would open doors for me, but my fear kept me defensive about this subject. I told myself that I didn't care about new opportunities and that I could achieve my goals without speaking in front of others. Once I overcame my fear I saw that this advice had been solid; new opportunities did come my way once I could speak on my topic in front of a group.

Early on I was encouraged to go to groups like Toastmasters to improve my speaking skills, but those groups were not a good fit for me. They were more concerned with the skill of public speaking and not the art of speaking publicly about what you know and love. There is a difference. Being able to share your message from the stage will empower you in a way that is impossible for me to adequately put into words.

Several years ago I found an acting teacher in Los Angeles who worked with public speakers as well as actors. For three months I attended his classes twice a week to learn how to feel more comfortable in front of an audience. Part of my goal was to be able to share more personal and emotional stories in front of a group without bursting into tears and feeling like I could not continue. These classes were perfect for what I wanted to achieve and my public speaking improved immensely over that time.

In 2009 I co-hosted my first live Internet marketing event with Dr. Jeanette Cates. This was also a turning point in my life as I realized the power of gathering people together in order to teach them what they yearn to know.

When I think about this further, I see that actually my first live event was one I co-hosted with another entrepreneur back in 2007. We rented a small venue and had about a dozen small business owners attend. It was a four hour workshop where we taught them about building credibility and visibility for their businesses through blogging and other online marketing activities. You can start small as well, and build up to larger events over time. Your own credibility will skyrocket when you do this with groups of people to share your knowledge and ideas.

Yes, everything I am discussing here can be quite uncomfortable at first. But like everything else in life it will become second nature as you continue to practice and improve. Writing was not comfortable to me at first, but with daily practice I turned myself into an author and have now written well over half a million words for my books, articles, blog posts, short reports, and information products. Speaking was even more uncomfortable because I couldn't hide behind my computer, but regular practice continues to improve that as well. Be willing to experiment with new things and your life will change. Choose to do this not because it is easy, but because it is hard and that in doing so will set you apart from most of the people you will ever know.

Conclusion

Have a mind that is open to everything and
attached to nothing. ~ Tilopa

As with my previous eleven books, this book has been a joy to write. Taking an idea from conception through birth can feel like an arduous task, but once your ideas begin to unfold and you think about the people who will be served by the information you are sharing it all falls into place.

My challenge to you is to spend some time every single day working on an aspect of your business using one or more of the three prongs I have introduced here. Find the joy in planning a post you will write and publish to your block, shooting a three minute video to post to YouTube, and adding more to the outline for your book. Know that with each action, no matter how small or seemingly insignificant it may feel at the time, you are moving closer to your overall goal of building a successful and lucrative online business.

Share what you are doing with your family and friends as soon as possible, but only after you have taken the time to flesh out your ideas into a workable plan. Sharing too soon can open the doors to self doubt, and you do not need that. Be ready to field questions and concerns as to what you are attempting, as this will be good practice in the future. The people close to us simply want to protect us from harm, and your excitement may signal danger in their subconscious mind. That's okay. Your actions over time will say much more than any words you can conjure up in the very beginning of this journey.

Read through this book completely at two different times. I have found that once is never enough when it comes to information sticking in your brain. The first time through is typically what I refer to as a 'quick read', while the second time is more of a deep dive into information being assimilated into the core of your being. If you found yourself skipping around the first time, go chapter by chapter the second time around. Take notes, implement something new you have learned, think about it, and come back to read more. This will truly be the path of least resistance and will help you to achieve your goals.

Do not be afraid to ask for help. I mistakenly believed that I had to personally know how to do everything my new online business would require in order to get it up and running. I quickly learned that technology and graphics were not my areas of strength and that it made perfect sense to outsource those tasks to others. I don't cut my own hair or change the oil in my car, so why would I ever feel like I had to spend the time and make the effort to learn do those things in my business that could better be accomplished by others?

It's the same with your new business. Becoming an entrepreneur means that you will spend the time learning and doing the things you enjoy and have some talent for and nothing else. I like to think of it in this way: if I do something that I am not good at and do not enjoy, I am taking that task away from someone who is and does.

Write everything down as you go through your day. As your mind expands so will your thoughts, so you'll want to keep a record of your ideas, insights, and goals. I keep a notebook in my purse, have another one in my car, and also have one in my office. Some of these ideas have turned into lucrative business ventures, while others have led me to changing my path on something I initially thought was the right direction for me.

Most of all, believe in yourself every single day. Practice positive self talk and pat yourself on the back for every little thing you do. This advice can be worth a fortune over time. Becoming an entrepreneur is a worthwhile goal and one that most people will not entertain for longer than a second or two. Staying the path and improving your mind and your circumstances will give you the greatest sense of joy and accomplishment you will ever experience.

Even though no man is an island, this is something you must do on your own to begin with. Make a promise to yourself to work hard and to not give up. I experienced this in my own journey, as I was so frustrated during that first year and came so close to giving up a number of times. Instead, I persevered and continued to learn and implement everything I could to make at least some progress every single day. It paid off in a big way as my actions compiled into huge returns on my time investment.

Recently I was speaking with my friend, acclaimed copywriter Michael Fortin, about this very topic. He says that he continues to learn from his students and clients and that doing the work propels him forward in his own business. He recounted the time back in 2009 when he and his late wife, Sylvie spent a day with me going through my business with a fine toothed comb. It was so uncomfortable for me the first few minutes, but once I let down my defenses and became open and vulnerable to what they had to share with me everything turned around. They benefitted as well by learning what my thought process had been while I was creating and setting up various aspects of my business.

Stay open to constructive criticism and allow it to help you move through the process of growth in a positive way. And as the quote I opened this section with from the tenth century Indian tantric practitioner Tilopa says, have a mind that is open to everything and attached to nothing.

Resources

*A single conversation with a wise man during the
eating of a meal, is better than ten
years' mere study of books.*
~ *Chinese Proverb*

These are some resources to help you get your business
started right away.

My most recent teleseminar:
http://AskConnieAnything.com

My main sites:
http://ConnieRagenGreen.com
http://HugeProfitsTinyList.com

My other books:
http://ConnieRagenGreenBooks.com

Hosting:
http://BlueHostSolutions.com

History of WordPress:
https://en.wikipedia.org/wiki/WordPress

Tilopa: https://en.wikipedia.org/wiki/Tilopa

Book. Blog. Broadcast.

Lesson Plan:
http://www.lausd.k12.ca.us/Carlson_Hospital_School/PDF%20files/LessonPlanDesign.pdf

Autoresponder E-Course:
http://AutoresponderEcourse.com

Autoresponder Service:
http://ConnieLoves.me/Aweber

John F. Kennedy's 'We Choose to go to the Moon' speech:
https://en.wikipedia.org/wiki/We_choose_to_go_to_the_Moon

About the Author

Connie Ragen Green is a bestselling author of a dozen books, an international speaker, and an online marketing strategist working with clients on six continents to help them build lucrative online businesses. After getting off to a slow start in 2006 because of challenges with writing and technology, Connie went on to build a business she can run from anywhere in the world she happens to be.

Making her home in both the desert community of Santa Clarita, California and the beachside community of Santa Barbara, California, Connie splits her time between the two cities as well as traveling the world for business and pleasure.

She is dedicated to helping new online entrepreneurs to live by design, and to change their lives forever.

Made in the USA
San Bernardino, CA
04 October 2015